Praise for

WHEN YOUR MIRACLE *Doesn't Come*

Jacki exemplifies what it means to turn your obstacles into opportunities. In her book, she invites readers to shift their perspectives of their struggles, helping them find hope, courage, and the strength to keep moving forward. For anyone going through a challenging time or having a hard time getting through something from the past, this book is for you! Jacki's own story of choosing strength over struggle is sure to inspire you and help you along your own journey.

Alexa Rose Carlin
Bestselling Author of *Adaptable*

The resiliency of The Corta Family is a quality I've long admired. Doug, Jacki, Z, Demi, and Bentli are amazing people, and *When Your Miracle Doesn't Come* will finally reveal to the world why. For as long as I've known them, they've attacked adversity together with grace, even when the circumstances were grim. It's something that's been hard for me to comprehend... up until now.

I know their story. I've told their story. But when reflecting upon their struggle, it's often left me pondering: *How did they get through this?*

Anyone that's met Jacki knows she is a loving mom. She is also tough, authentic, passionate, humble, kind, and caring.

Now she reveals her talents as a writer. *When Your Miracle Doesn't Come* takes you turn by turn on a remarkably difficult journey, as Jacki's one true love battles an unstoppable opponent: brain cancer.

She does it all while being a wife, mother, caregiver, coach, and provider.

You will look at life differently after reading this book. Jacki offers gripping advice on how and ways to stay present and appreciate what you have, rather than focusing on circumstances you deem unfair or incidences you can't control.

You can wait for a miracle to happen to you, or you can control your response to adversity and, hopefully, your strength can be a miracle for someone else who is feeling overwhelmed or grieving.

Doug and Jacki will be that miracle for anyone who reads this book.

I got to experience the magical connection between them. It was—and still is—love personified. I wholeheartedly believe he is smiling down from above as proud as ever of his endearing wife, and three amazing daughters.

Jay Tust
Sports Director, Anchor

Jacki Corta tells a story that reflects a boldness in the face of adversity that the world needs. She candidly shares the good, the bad, and the extremes of the grief that come with a cancer diagnosis. A death story before death. Her reflections of holding in the storm bring freedom and healing to those heart sick with grief.

Rachel Faulkner Brown
Founder of Be Still Ministries and Never Alone Widows
Author of *His Name* and co author of *Father's House Bible Study*

Jacki invites you into her raw story of strength that brings readers to a unique level of faith. She doesn't hold back her heart as she tells you about many difficult moments of her family's unexpected journey with cancer. This perspective comes from a heart full of gratitude and carries you through with hope, no matter your struggles. You will be encouraged by scriptures and wisdom that God revealed in this hard season for the Corta family.

Nick Toves
Pastor, Author, Miracle Worker

The Corta family's story is one of inspirational courage through insurmountable circumstances; exemplifying their overcoming journey through struggle to strength. Jacki's perseverance and perspective will penetrate your heart, taking you on a real-life pathway through laughter and tears. Hold tight & lean in as Jacki's testimony of faith collides with your story; I am confident you will be beautifully impacted!

Jeremy DeFrees,
Worship Pastor and Family Friend

WHEN YOUR
MIRACLE
Doesn't Come

HOLDING ON TO
FAITH, HOPE, AND STRENGTH
THROUGH THE STRUGGLE

jacki corta

Edited by Laurie Knight
Cover Design by: Kristina Edstrom

An Imprint for GracePoint Publishing (www.GracePointPublishing.com)

GracePoint Matrix, LLC
624 S. Cascade Ave, Suite 201
Colorado Springs, CO 80903
www.GracePointMatrix.com
Email: Admin@GracePointMatrix.com

SAN # 991-6032

Library of Congress Control Number 2023941542

ISBN: (Paperback) 978-1-955272-99-5
eISBN: 978-0-9724686-8-8

Books may be purchased for educational, business, or sales promotional use.
For bulk order requests and price schedule contact:
Orders@GracePointPublishing.com

To my dear Douglas. Thank you for believing in me, always having my back and co-writing one of the best love stories a girl could ask for. Love you… Promise!

1 Timothy 4:7

I have fought the good fight, I have finished the race, I have kept the faith.

Table of Contents

Foreward

I met Jacki through what some might call social media coincidence, though there is no word in the Hebrew language for coincidence. It was appointed, long before there were stars in the skies and water in the vast oceans. I know that we were drawn to each other by loss and ultimately triumph through grief. Because what I know about grief is that there is never a getting over it, it's the fire alarm missing the battery at three in the morning. When it wants to announce itself, it will. You have to learn how to triumph in the midst of it. You have to learn how to live with it.

Jacki has boldly turned her pain into her purpose, her mess into her message. While grief is something we have all faced or must face, rarely do we see someone pull pearls from their pigsty like Jacki has. It is an amazing feat of enduring love, faith, and hope that formed the path allowing her and her family to walk through grief with grace.

What happens when your miracle doesn't come? You learn to see the miracles in the other things around you. You learn to find your miracles, to view your life as a miracle, and to know that miracles are coming that you don't even know about yet. Jacki teaches us that the miracle that doesn't come in the way you wanted, in the way you thought or hoped it would, is still a purposeful moment.

Come along with her on this journey of self-discovery, joy, pain, loss, and ultimately bold purpose. You will be better for having read these pages. Grab your tissues, your journal, and your book club for this amazing journey of a book.

Rachel Joy Baribeau,
Author of Relentless Joy and
Founder of www.ImChangingtheNarrative.org

Introduction

Miracle

Definition: A surprising and welcome event that is not explicable by natural or scientific laws and is therefore considered to be the work of a divine agency.

A highly improbable or extraordinary event, development, or accomplishment that brings very welcome consequences.

An amazing product or achievement or an outstanding example of something.

I always knew someone would gain something from my story. Knowing one soul would benefit from hearing my tale was the motivation I needed to finish writing *When Your Miracle Doesn't Come*. I had a goal of sharing the journey my husband and I faced, believing the ways we faced adversity and handled our experiences were the key ingredients to help others overcome the struggles in their own lives.

My hope for this writing is for the experiences to embolden each reader into conquering whatever they may face on their own journeys. I want readers to find hope in their own stories, even in the most difficult and heartbreaking of circumstances.

Much of the power and hope I held along my path with Doug and his cancer came from prayer and God. A connection to anything beyond the self is a valuable thing and one that I hope each reader will be open to even if the connection to a higher power is not the same as the connection I have to the Lord. I ask my readers to be open-minded, have grace, and see what messages are coming through my own journey and these pages.

When Your Miracle Doesn't Come holds messages of strength, resilience, hope, and faith through the most difficult struggles. I hope the messages land well and help in the journey or plant a small seed which will reap a huge harvest one day.

Much of my experience and the writing in this book is raw, and I speak from truth and the heart. Some of our most vulnerable moments are those with the most value, and I wish to share even if only one soul may experience the light in their darkness. I want to tell how we chose to walk it out and how I learned my strength is greater than my struggle, which is what I later turned into a brand (Strength > Struggle™) for empowering others to be their best and overcome their hardships.

There is value in the experience I wish to bring forward in this book. I ask my readers to not only read the words but also to *feel* their impact and the impact each experience had on me and my family as we lived through one of the darkest times in our lives.

I have sat in prayer that my story will get to exactly the souls that need it. My hope is that each person holding it or listening to it on audio realizes it is not an accident. This is divine timing. This is going to be a phenomenal experience, and I ask that my readers embrace the hard.

When something difficult arrives in life, there is a challenge in it. My wish is that the experience of this book is also a form of challenge to the way each reader experiences their own stories and difficulties. I hope my readers question how they are facing the situations and experiences of their own lives. I hope they consider whether they are being graceful with themselves and others and if they are seeing the good in their situations. I hope they look at whether they are willing to fight for their miracles and whether they are trusting God. The way forward is one full of choice and question, and I also hope my story and the path through it is one which inspires others to also live in a way that will create inspiration.

I am blessed beyond measure that the Lord has chosen me to share my story with the world. The only thing I have ever wanted out of this was to help one person. My family and I knew if our story could help, then we had done it for good and the ripple effect would occur. At this point in my journey, inspiring others with our story is the greatest miracle of all.

When Your Miracle Doesn't Come is full of incredible miracles which, at the time, we were unable see. Miracles are happening all around, but they may not look the way people expect or hope for. That is as much the case for my family as it is for anyone.

With hope, here is my journey, my truth, my challenges, my victories, and my heartfelt story on what happens if a miracle doesn't come exactly as planned.

Chapter One

2021

November 6, 2021, marked six years of living my life without Douglas. Six years. Six years filled with billions of tears that never cease. Six years of heartache. Six years of walking into the unknown. Six years of growth. Six years of finding the new normal.

I had no idea what the journey of grief would look like, and I had no idea how I would travel it. I did know I did not want to get stuck in it. I wanted to walk *through* it, or sit through it, exactly how I needed to, and I knew I would allow myself to take as long as I needed to heal. When your heart is in shattered pieces, still aching for the love of your life, and you are supporting your three young daughters as they yearn for the presence of their dad, you give yourself grace and permission to take as long as needed in the process.

The grief journey is one I could talk about for days—the things I experienced, learned, confronted, taught, gained, and witnessed. I will say it has been a rough road with many trials, lessons, setbacks, and victories. I believe grief is a roller coaster to ride for the rest of one's life.

There was a moment in my journey that caused a shift within me. I was attending an event and the speaker said, "Life is happening *for* you, not *to* you."

Wait, what? Throughout our story, we never played the victim; we always saw ourselves as the victors even when times were hard. But I stepped back as I heard that simple sentence again. *Life is happening for you, not to you.*

I quickly evaluated my forty-plus years of life and could see how this eight-word sentence was true. Just like when the warrior came out of me upon hearing of Doug's diagnosis, here emerged a stronger version of Jacki. I immediately was reminded of the impact we wanted to have by sharing our story, and I knew I was meant to continue sharing my story without Doug physically by my side.

In early 2018, I became an intuitive life coach. Then, toward the end of 2018, I lost my dad and quickly added grief coach to my résumé. I have been blessed to coach and speak life into others as I sit with them in their pain, giving them a space to share and teaching them how to implement the tools that worked so well for me. I have spoken on many stages, sharing my story in hopes of touching one soul.

I am on a mission to not only share my story but also my brand, Strength > Struggle™. I feel the Lord has given me this story to share with millions, encouraging, inspiring, planting seeds, and showing that no matter what—even when there is nothing else to hold on to—we can hold onto hope.

Cancer barged into my life and took my best friend, the love of my life, and the father of my three girls, but it also brought with it so many positive life lessons. It gave me courage. It showed me adversity and then it taught me how to overcome. It reminded me we were writing a love story, and I began to cherish it a bit more. It eloquently shared hardship and heartache, which forged a strength I had never known. It brought my faith to the forefront with a strong intent. It also showed me how short life is, and how we need to be living it fully. Every. Single. Day. It gave me a voice that will echo forever how good God is, along with showing me exactly what a miracle in my life looks like.

Miracles are not always the big healing we expect. In fact, miracles show up in all shapes and sizes. There are miracles in the lost folks who, through our story, came to know the Lord. There was a miracle evident in the way teenage boys approached Doug when he was physically weak—a deep sign of respect for the strength they saw in those otherwise fragile days. Miracles are the simplest acts of kindness that can change the direction of others' lives. There are miracles in the display of courage, bravery, and love that three sisters share. We can pray for a miracle, we can believe in a miracle, but what we need to realize is through each of our journeys, miracles are happening all around us—some we will never know about. The wonder and work of God is a daily activity… a miracle.

Romans 15:13

May the God of hope fill you with all joy and peace as you trust in him, so that you may overflow with hope by the power of the Holy Spirit.

Chapter Two

In the Beginning

Some time ago, a fifteen-year-old girl found herself falling in love with a man five-and-a-half years older. Although others thought she was crazy at that young age committing to such a serious relationship, she did not allow their opinions to influence her path. So, at nineteen years old she married her soulmate, her true love, the one and only.

I am so beyond grateful I listened to my heart, my soul, and what God was calling me to do. I truly had found the man I wanted to spend the rest of my life with.

I was a young sophomore in high school when this older boy, Doug, came into my life. There was a connection I look back on and can't explain. I knew I wanted to be with him.

I remember saying my prayers at night— "Lord guide me to the one I am supposed to be with. Guide me, Lord, to the one that I am to give my heart to."

Doug and I continued to date through my junior year. During my senior year, we had a difficult time and I wanted to enjoy that last year of high school. We broke up, got back together, broke up, and by the end of my senior year, we were back together, yet again.

After graduation, Doug did something that, to this day, I thank him for. He told me he loved me and wanted to spend the rest of his life with me but would not ask me to marry him until I got some sort of schooling behind me.

I knew I wanted to be a stylist, so I enrolled in beauty school in the fall. Ten months later I graduated, and a week after graduation Doug proposed to me on the beach in Seaside, Oregon at sunset. Eight months later, at the ripe age of nineteen, I married my best friend.

It was not always the fairy tale people hope for, but we began a life together that we thought would be years in the making. In January 1993, Doug opened the Burger Den in Eagle, and in March 1993, we were married.

A new business and a new marriage were a lot to handle for both of us, so why not add a baby to make it all better? In 1994, baby number one, Z, arrived. Then in our fourth year of marriage, baby number two, Bentli, arrived. Right after our seventh anniversary, Demi, baby number three was born. I was twenty-six and Doug was thirty-two.

As the years went by, we built a life of great contentment. The girls were growing up and we were starting to discuss what life was going to look like once we were empty nesters. I will never forget a conversation Douglas and I had one day as we drove to run errands. It was the where-has-time-gone conversation that led to me looking at him and saying, "We only have six years until Demi graduates."

I said, "Are you going to still like me? I know you love me, but it will be just the two of us then. Are you sure you will still like me?"

He giggled and replied, "If I wasn't going to like you, I would have already gotten rid of you!"

We both began to laugh, and I remember looking at him seriously and stating, "You, my dear, are stuck with me forever. I am not going anywhere... ever!"

Doug and I valued teamwork. We were always together—peas in a pod. I could hardly remember a time when it was just me or just Doug handling life's events.

Like any busy family, Doug and I had our challenges. We were at a stage of life where our daughters were old enough to get themselves ready and off to school. Our eldest daughter, Z, was away at college, and our afternoons and evenings continued to be filled with practices and games for the girls—Doug and I coaching softball and basketball respectively.

With Doug working at our restaurant early in the mornings, I spent those with the girls before heading to the salon. Due to our differing schedules, there were more times we saw each other in passing than we were together, which I believed to be normal. Everyone did what we were doing. I had watched my parents juggle it all while they were raising me. We were a normal, God-loving family of five. I never lacked time for Doug; it just hadn't been a priority since I knew I would see him as we lay down each night. And, luckily, we had downtime to recharge.

After a weekend in Ogden, Doug wasn't feeling well. He complained he couldn't shut his mind off. I took him to urgent care where they checked his blood pressure, told us he was probably having anxiety, and urged us to follow up with the doctor the following day.

That next morning, Doug called me and asked me to take him to the doctor. I knew he wasn't feeling well because he asked *me* to take him. Typically, if he was sick, I wouldn't even know or would only notice because he was more needy or resting. Doctors were never involved when it came to Doug.

His doctor diagnosed him with anxiety and depression and prescribed an antidepressant and anxiety meds, but by Thursday, Doug was having severe headaches. Thinking it was a side effect of the antidepressant, he stopped taking it and his headaches went away.

A few days later, we talked to his doctor and had his antidepressant changed. Not long after, he started to get another headache, and it quickly became so severe he began throwing up.

I rushed him to urgent care where they did a few blood pressure tests and told us we needed to rule out possibilities before they would send him home. But that meant going to the ER.

So off we went to the hospital downtown. They started an IV and administered a migraine cocktail through it. The pain went away, but the ER doctor said they wanted to do a CT scan of his head to rule out anything major.

I sat in the room while he was getting the scan, praying fervently. After a few minutes, Doug returned and then we got the news. I should have known when two doctors and a nurse came in together, they were not there to tell me he's ready to go home and all is fine!

The doctor told us that on the scan it showed a two-inch spot/lesion on the right side of his brain.

I'm a no-BS gal; I want it all up front, don't hold back. So, I said, "Is it a tumor?"

The response I got was, "A CT scan shows a spot/lesion, and he is scheduled for an MRI in the morning." They gave Doug a steroid to help with the pressure in his head. Then they walked out of the room to get the discharge papers.

I sat next to the bed and held Doug's hand. I told him, "This is not going to take us down. We will find out what it is, and we are going to fight. We will fight to win this battle."

Honestly, all I could do was hold it together. Facing the possibilities felt terrifying and I didn't *want* to know if it was bad news. Words like *cancer* and *tumor* were more than I wanted to think about, but they jumped to the front of my thoughts faster than I could stop them. Those fears were not strong enough to take me down though. I saw a vulnerability I had never seen before in my husband, and I knew I needed to be strong for him.

He looked me in the eyes and softly spoke, "I want to go home."

At that moment I knew he was worried.

I also knew I was scared as well, but knew I had to withhold my emotions and help hold my husband up. This was the beginning of the strength that would carry us through.

As we drove home, I put the girls on a three-way call.

"Hello?"

"Bent, is Demi with you?"

"Yeah."

"Put me on speakerphone and let me get Z on here."

"Hello?"

"Hey sis, I have Bent and Demi on here as well."

Three different hellos to each other, and I continued.

"The scan shows there is a spot, and it's on Dad's brain…"

Sobs began to fill the conversation.

"He is scheduled for an MRI in the morning."

"Mom, what do you mean a spot?" Bentli asked.

"Sis, they called it a spot or lesion that needs further looking at before they can determine what it is."

"Is it cancer?"

"They won't know until they do the MRI, then we should have more answers."

Silence, sniffles, and a small argument to pull it together was heard on the other end.

Z asked, "Mom, how is Dad?"

"He is better since they gave him some meds. We are headed home now."

There was complete silence for what felt like five minutes.

"Girls, it is natural to feel scared and have tears."

I could hear more crying and Z whispered, "Mom I'm going to go."

"Okay sis, I'll keep you posted. Love you."

"Love you Mom, tell Dad I love him."

"Absolutely!"

"Bye."

"Bye sis."

With that hang up Bent said, "Mom, we are going to go too."

"Okay sis, we will be home soon. Love you girls."

"Love you too."

There was not much conversation when we arrived home. Doug was exhausted.

The next day we walked into the clinic where he would have his MRI.

"Jack, will you stay with me during the MRI?"

"Sweets, if they will let me, yes I will stay with you."

We checked him in and waited.

A familiar voice said, "Doug?"

As I looked up, I noticed the MRI tech was Bentli's friend's mom.

"How are you guys?" she asked as we walked through the door toward the MRI room.

"Could be better," Doug said.

I began small talk. "How have you been? It is so good to see you." With a slight pause in my voice, I asked, "Doug would really like me to go in with him during the scan. Is there any way I can be with him?"

"We will make it happen for you."

As we walked into the room, goose bumps appeared all over from the chill of the room. Doug was placed on the table that would roll into the tube where he would be scanned for about an hour.

"Jacki, you can stand here next to his legs."

"Can I touch him while he is in?"

"Yes," turning to Doug, "as long as you can hold still with her touching you."

We all had a small giggle, as we both put earplugs in.

I looked down at Doug, gave him a kiss and said, "I am right here with you; you are not doing this alone."

She slowly slid him back into the tube as a flashback of a scene from the movie *Days of Thunder* ran through my head. I settled my hands on his legs and I prayed. As the time passed, I massaged his legs, letting him be reminded I was still there.

At one point my mind began to wonder. There I was, standing in a very cold room watching my husband have an MRI on his brain to determine what the spot was. Staring down with a slight glance into the tube, I could feel a lump form in my throat. *What are we going to be facing?* I finally cried. I was scared!

The following day, we met with the neurosurgeon. Nerves were unsteady as we waited in the room for the doctor in hopes we would get some answers on what the spot/lesion was. I felt my heart sink with the creaking of the door.

"Good afternoon. How are you doing, Doug?" asked the doctor.

"Okay."

"Let's check some things." Doug stood and followed along with all of the doctor's seemingly unrelated and random requests. "Hold your arms up. Now close your eyes but keep your arms up. Good. I would like you to walk a straight line, heel to toe."

I didn't notice any wavering in his ability to do all the things asked of him.

I sat there curious and confused about what this had to do with the scan.

Oddly still, the doctor continued, "One last thing, Doug, take your fingers and one by one touch your thumb and then do it in reverse for me."

In my not-so-professional opinion, Doug did all the testing very well. The neurosurgeon then sat down on a small stool and began to tell us about his findings from the MRI.

Without any hesitation or prep, he continued, "The scan shows you have an unknown brain tumor located in a sensitive spot of your brain."

I could feel the energy shift in the room as he continued.

"We will need to schedule surgery…"

Questions and thoughts overtook me. *Is this cancer? How long is surgery? What is the downtime to heal? How many days in the hospital? Is Doug okay hearing this news? How will we tell the girls? I need to get my prayer warriors on this.* Not knowing what I'd missed, and hoping it wasn't much, I became present in the conversation again.

"… within the next week. The surgery will be a three-to-five-hour procedure to remove the tumor. Once we have removed it, we will send it to pathology to be tested. Then we will know what we are dealing with."

Doug quietly asked, "Is it cancer?"

My heart sank because I was *not* going there. Although the thought ran through my head, I had not prepared myself to hear the C word. Mentally, I needed to have things in order so fear didn't take over. *Let's get through the surgery before we start shouting out that word!*

With the most confident voice, the doctor looked at both Doug and me and stated, "I do not believe this is cancer, the shaping of it is not in form with cancer tumors. But we will know for sure once we have surgery."

Once we loaded in the pickup, I grabbed Doug's hand. "Are you okay?"

"I guess," he replied, unconvincingly.

"Douglas, I do not think we tell anyone that the doctor does not think it is cancer." I paused as I sought the words to carefully tiptoe into a topic that even I didn't want to consider. "If we tell the girls and then it turns out to be, which we are believing it isn't, they will be even more devastated."

"I agree, Jack, let's just see what surgery shows." He turned to look out the window to perhaps protect me from seeing his immediate concern.

"Sweets, it's going to be okay," I offered as I internally summoned up strength to find optimism.

"I hope so, Jack." His reply showed me that his thoughts were shuffling as quickly as mine.

With a tight squeeze of his hand, I said, "It will be. Love you!"

"Love you too." And his hand loosened but remained in mine, devoid of any indication of where his thoughts had gone.

The unknown was still so present in my mind. So much was going to change, but not actually knowing what was changing or how dramatic it would be brought up feelings I wasn't ready to face.

I began thinking logically about what a surgery—any surgery—entails: hospitalization, procedure, recovery, and all the while, our regular schedules would have to be on hold. *How can I manage the girls' activities, the house, my jobs? Who will take care of the restaurant?* I pushed it all aside as best I could and simply acknowledged that recovery would shift our daily routines. Holding onto the rest of the emotions within was going to be tiresome, but I would have to keep it together for my girls and Doug. In my mind, if I showed any fear, it would only strengthen their fear. So, I kept my anxiousness trapped inside to protect those around me.

Thankfully, I had my faith, and I could cry out to God. He would be my comfort. I knew and felt deep in my being that through God all things were possible!

Chapter Three

Here We Go...
Meltdown Number One

I finally hit a wall one night. I knew it was coming, but crap, I had no idea I would hit it as hard as I did.

The stress of figuring out what neurosurgeon to use took over. It was nice to hear all the referrals of doctors from friends who had either used them or had heard they were good, but it was overwhelming. I had great information, but why couldn't I decide?

I was questioning from whom to seek a second opinion when I became paralyzed, feeling like a wall had just sprung up out of nowhere! Was it the pressure I was feeling to get it that pushed me to hit the wall? Was it the pressure I was feeling from so many people about it? I was trying to understand what we were facing along with a cyclone of emotions about a second opinion.

I sat in battle with myself for the whole evening when I decided to reach out for help and called my aunt. I grabbed my cell phone and touched each number with tears dripping onto the screen.

"Hey, Jack!"

Silence stood on my end; I couldn't speak.

"Jack, are you there?"

A sniffle escaped as she responded, "Are things okay?"

I quietly spoke, "How do I pick a neurosurgeon? What do I look for? What do I even ask? Doug has entrusted me to *know* which surgeon to use, and I am completely at a loss about it."

The best part of our conversation and what brought me the most comfort while I was bawling my eyes out was her response: "Jack, I have no advice for you. All I can tell you is you have a huge support group around you loving on you and Doug and those girls."

That is what I needed to hear, no BS! As I hung up the phone, I sat back down at the computer still trying to wrap my head around the whole doctor choice. It threw me into another crying fit. *Oh crap, that's meltdown number two!*

As I sat there crying, I decided to pray for guidance on my choice. I asked that we be blessed with the doctor that was the right fit for us. As I said amen, I noticed I had a message on Facebook from our youth pastor's wife. This is the first part of the message: "I read your Caring Bridge post, and my heart felt at peace when I saw you had the same neurosurgeon we had through my brother's brain injury, and I really felt he did a good job."

This was what I was yearning for. I needed to feel as if God was presenting me with the path to the exact neurosurgeon we needed. It was a small miracle.

Since Doug wasn't driving, I did everything with him. It took some rearranging of my schedule to get all the things I normally do done and to get him to his responsibilities and appointments. This time together I knew I would never get back, so I embraced it. He had difficulty staying focused, so I was there to keep him on task.

Among the many other responsibilities to schedule, we had a meeting at the high school to get all the softball team details in line for the other coaches. Doug was feeling very blessed for his loving and caring boss. She was so good to him. He was in an emotional stage, so he wanted to stop and see everyone on campus, tell them hi, and thank them for everything they were doing to help.

I gently guided him out the door or he would have hunted down all the custodians too! There was a moment as he was hugging and thanking some of the staff that it occurred to me—I felt like he was saying his final goodbyes. It brought a lump to my throat when a hug was shared, and I witnessed a very strong man shed tears as he thanked Doug.

We went home for a nap and then back to the high school for softball practice. He was at the high school for about four hours that day, and yes, he overdid it. I came into the house, and he was on the bed in the dark. When I asked him if he was okay, he began to cry.

I lay there with him, telling him it was okay to cry, and if he needed to, just to do it. This is when I realized, again, I had to pull up my big-girl panties, stuff my fears and insecurities, and be the strong one. As I recalled all the times he had been my strength and my rock, I acknowledged it was my turn to be his.

When we marry, a union of two hearts, we face challenges and struggles. It will take one holding the other up through the struggle. This was my time to be the one holding him up.

James 1:2-4

> *Consider it pure joy, my brothers, whenever you face trials of many kinds, because you know that the testing of your faith develops perseverance. Perseverance must finish its work so that you may be mature and complete, not lacking anything.*

Once we learned of the tumor and Douglas was put on steroid meds for the swelling, I noticed he was more tired. He seemed afraid at times. Brain surgery is no joke, and I knew the risks, but I was relying on my faith to keep me strong.

Doug looked me in the eyes and asked, "I'm so tired. Will it always be like this? Am I going to be back to myself? I want to have energy to do whatever I want to do." His vulnerability caused me to steel my own resolve.

Not having the perfect answer, I placed my hand on his cheek and spoke, "We are taking this in baby steps, and whatever the outcome, whatever we are about to face, it is going to be fine."

Fine is an interesting word. It usually pacifies the recipient. I immediately battled in my head, *Will it, Jack? Will it really be fine, or are you using* fine *to cover up your fear?*

Staying strong was my priority for Doug. I recognized that it was not the time for me to express the concerns and unease I was feeling with everything.

With tears running down his face, he said, "Will the doctor do a good job? Will he know what to do? I know I can recover, but I hate not being able to make sure he does a good job."

While I had those same concerns and was feeling deeply helpless, a small voice from deep inside urged me to rely on faith.

I held him and said, "Douglas, this is where we let go of control and hand it over to God. He is the ultimate healer; He is in control and will do us no wrong. Have faith that the Lord will lay His hands on you and bring healing."

Doug turned to me and said, "Now I see why the girls say what they say. How do you always know what to say, Jack?"

I smiled and gave him a kiss on the cheek, repeating those same words to myself until I felt them.

The following morning, I called and got the surgery scheduled and paperwork sent over. The fine details of paperwork and appointments would have caused havoc on Douglas, so it was up to me to get it done.

I learned through that process what life really means to me. We go through our daily hustle and bustle and forget what we are blessed with. Doug's illness put my life into perspective. It saddened me that it had taken something like brain surgery to make me step back and look at how I was living my life, how I had been living my life, and how I would be living my life moving forward.

I had been going through the motions of life. Running through each day getting where I or the girls needed to be. I had fallen into a routine with the day-to-day. But in this new routine where I was my husband's constant companion, caregiver, scheduler, driver, and pep-talk coach, I had not taken the time to see the beauty surrounding me or even the amazing souls who were doing life with me.

Because we were facing an unknown, I saw I needed to slow down a bit, to not allow the smallest things to get to me, and to see the good in everything. It was teaching me to acknowledge the blessings that were in my everyday life even when it felt like a bad day.

Why do we wait? Why does it take a crisis to send us into thankfulness? Is it human nature? Are we scared to share our feelings? Are we afraid it won't be accepted? Do we think people know?

Whatever the reasons, it is hard for me to understand. I know from having gone through this process, I will be a bit more thankful, more grateful, more kind, more understanding, and I will show more compassion to others. I am not waiting for those people to be in a crisis any longer.

Thinking back to how I've grown, I now feel the need to reach out to everyone and take a moment to thank them, tell them I love them, and tell them how they have impacted my life and the lives of my family members. I want everyone to know how much I truly care about them.

At that time, Doug had received so many kind and loving words since receiving the news of the tumor. That small support was enough to brighten our most difficult days.

I was reminded of the smallest things that deserve gratitude, like breath in my lungs and waking up in the mornings with people I love lying next to me or in the next room over. Upheaval brings a clarity to the simple things in life we need to be grateful for. I found myself grateful for the roof over our head, the food in our pantry, the loved ones helping, and the wisdom of the doctors. I wanted to do my best to not take the simple things for granted anymore.

Through this, I began discovering grace. I gave myself the grace only the Lord could give me and saw how I could spread more grace to others and to our situation.

I was doing my absolute best with the circumstances we were facing and traveling the path of the unknown no matter how scary that path looked.

Chapter Four

The Day Before

CaringBridge Entry
March 12, 2014

It's been a roller coaster of a ride today. Prayers were felt when my knees became too weak to hold me up. I know those who love and support us were holding us in that scary time. My heart has been sad and scared, scared, *scared*! I think it is natural to feel so afraid, at least I hope it is.

Doug went to have blood work done today, and when the nurse came to take him to get his blood drawn, Doug said to her, "Don't be shocked if it's green with a hint of purple! See, I bleed green with a hint of purple, but might be more purple in time!"

Those are the colors that represent his softball team and Z's college team.

I went and spoke to the softball team for him today. I wanted to inform them of what was going on with Doug, their coach, but more importantly I wanted to speak to them on staying focused on their game and not on what was happening off the field. I needed to remind them that sometimes life challenges us similarly to the game they play, but we stay on track with what we know, and we don't allow things we can't control to consume us. I let them know that the drills they have done thousands of times are so they can make the plays instantaneously, without even thinking, and that they should keep playing their best. Being distracted over what is happening to their beloved coach will not help them and it certainly wouldn't help him.

Those girls are a special bunch of young ladies.

I usually drive in silence, but this day I was drawn to turn the radio on and the song "From the Inside Out" was playing. A section of the song pierced my soul as it talked about giving the Lord control to consume from the inside out. I felt His presence like no other, for I have Him right here next to me.

Knowing He is next to me gives me strength while I keep everyone informed on what the next steps are. It is an exhausting task, and I feel relief when I rely on Him—when I allow Him to help hold it, and me, up.

There have been a lot of discussions between Doug and our girls the past couple of days. With Z off at college playing softball in Utah and Bent and Demi playing for the high school softball team here in Idaho, we had to decide who would be at the hospital the day of surgery. Z has a game in San Diego playing in a collegiate tournament while Bent and Demi have opening day on their home field.

Doug was adamant they needed to be on the softball field; that is where he wanted them.

The phone call was made to Z.

"Hello?"

"Hey sis, how's your day going?"

"Mom, is Dad okay?"

"Oh gosh, yes, sorry. I wanted to let you know surgery has been scheduled for March 13th. I know you have games in California that day. Dad is sitting here next to me, and he wants you playing, not here sitting at the hospital."

There was silence on the other end of the phone. In all reality, I cannot imagine the strain she must have felt.

"Mom, I think I will come home. Let me talk to Coach."

Not wanting to argue or push in either direction, I acquiesced with a simple, "Sounds good."

In time and with much back and forth, all three girls made the decision to play their games, but I had strict orders to keep them updated on Dad.

I am not sure this is the decision I would have made had it been solely up to me. Doug felt so strongly they needed to not be at the hospital that it outweighed what I felt. In my heart, I wanted them at the hospital in case something went wrong. *Am I really doubting the success of the surgery?*

Softball is such an intense mental game, and it worried me they may not be present and focused enough on the field. I could not pressure them to be at the hospital, and I was not telling them to play. I had to be neutral. It concerned me they may regret not being at the hospital, and Z would be hundreds of miles away, but ultimately, it had to be the girls' decision.

Chapter Five

The Battle Begins

Surgery went well. It was the longest four hours of my life as I sat there in prayer and in fear waiting for Doug to get out of surgery.

The operating room waiting area was full of family and friends; I was not going to tell anyone they couldn't come to the hospital. It was slightly overwhelming having everyone there, but I understood why they were.

I wanted my space and needed no one to talk to me. I wanted to initiate conversation *if* I wanted it. The chair was not comfortable as I sat there with earbuds blaring worship music. In four hours, I took many walks to a quiet courtyard to get fresh air, always carrying the pager that would notify me when Doug was out of surgery.

The concern from each family member that circulated the waiting room was almost too much to take. I went and sat in the courtyard with my cousin. I decided early on that I would be the only one to go back to speak with the neurosurgeon, but as I felt the breeze hit my face and watched a small bird walk within inches of me, there was a shift.

As if God spoke directly to me, my decision changed to having Doug's dad, mom, sister, and my mom go back to hear what the neurosurgeon had to say about the surgery. I recognized how I needed others to hear what the team would tell us, not only for my own support, but also to help keep straight any news or information that I may have trouble processing.

The moment came. A nurse announced all our names and walked us back to the small room. She recognized my anxiety and looked at me, encouraging me to take deep breaths as she walked me back with the family trailing behind.

As we all sat there, the nurse told us it would be about fifteen minutes before the doctor came in. As we each sat, our thoughts racing and expressions as blank as possible, we waited. That fifteen minutes felt like a lifetime!

I sat in silence praying as hard as I could pray. As the time went on, my heart began to race. It felt like it was going to beat right out of my chest. I think the nerves were getting the best of all of us, but I simply sat in the chair staring into the hallways, gazing at nothing.

I said to the four that were in there with me, "It was up to me on who I brought into this meeting, and I pondered coming by myself. Then I flipped the situation on myself and realized if my daughter or sister was the one having brain surgery, there is no building, doctor, or mountain that would keep me from being in this room. I knew I had to bring you all. You all deserve to be here."

I could see gratitude on the faces of my family members. In all honesty, their expressions let me know I made the right decision. Plus, it helped me to have extra people there in case I missed some of the information the doctor had to say. It felt better to know I had people there who loved us and would do everything for Doug if anything bad should come from surgery.

As the neurosurgeon walked in, he looked as if he had been crying. He looked me straight in the eyes and said, "Surgery went well. Doug did really good."

I could feel a huge *but* coming. And then it did.

Without hesitation he added, "But the tumor itself was a malignant tumor."

Everyone in the room began to cry. I stayed stone-faced. *Was it shock?* Looking back, I now believe it was the warrior strength that had instantly engrossed every ounce of my being. I shifted gears and began asking questions; I knew I must prepare for battle.

Will we have the final report on Monday? Will he need chemo and radiation? I looked the neurosurgeon in the eyes and could only say, "Wow! Wow! Wow! I did not expect that." Internally, I had held onto his words at the office where he did not think the tumor was cancerous. My hope was for a benign tumor, as he'd indicated earlier, and now that hope was dashed. *How can I do this?*

"Neither did I," he returned.

I thanked him for taking such good care of Doug, and he said he would continue to do so. As he gave me a hug, tears filled his eyes.

I went through the feeling of *What has God handed me?* I sat in a quiet room, silently pondering how to tell my three young girls that their dad has cancer. I began to shake, and chills ran up my body.

As I walked into Doug's room in the intensive care unit, he lay there with a bandage on his head and his eyes softly closed. He felt my presence, and with his eyes cracked open said, "How did it go?"

I calmly said, "Really well, he got 90 percent of the tumor, the other he could not get because of the position and his concern of it affecting your left side."

With worry in his voice, he said, "Jack, is it going to be okay?"

I told him, "Yep. We have a battle ahead of us but we both decided whatever it was, we were going to fight to win." There was a pause and I continued, "It was cancer, and we're going to have a final report on Monday. We are going to battle through this. Together."

He closed his eyes as I kissed his cheek. I whispered, "You rest, my love."

Z was in San Diego playing softball, and I was concerned about telling her over the phone. I made the call to her coach instead.

"Hello?"

"Hey Coach, it's Jacki."

"Hi, we have Z right here with us."

"Okay, thanks." I paused, wondering just how to tell her.

"Hey Mom." She said it so innocently I was reminded of her as a young child.

Not knowing how to say such news and having not had to say it yet, I faltered. I started with small talk. I asked, "Hi sis, how were your games?"

"They were fine, Mom. How's Dad?" It's never been like Z to want to sit with the mundane for long.

"He is doing good; he is resting in his room. He is sleepy still." I hoped she wouldn't ask more since we didn't have much more except cancer following a successful surgery.

"What did they say it was?" *I should have known she would press for more. At least her coaches are there. I have to be strong. I must tell her what I know.*

A lump in my throat began to form. "Sis, it is cancer." *Keep talking so she doesn't have a chance to say anything.* "The neurosurgeon feels he got 90 percent of the tumor. They are sending tissue to pathology, and we should have those results in a few days."

The typical Z came out, the strong young lady she has always been. I could hear a quiver in her voice as she said, "Tell Dad I love him."

"Absolutely, sis, I will tell him."

"Love you Mom," she murmured and then her coach was back on the phone.

I quickly explained everything to her coach.

She could feel my concern through the phone as she replied, "I have her. We will take good care of her."

"Please give her a hug for me. Thanks Coach."

As I hit the end button on my cell phone, tears began to build from the ache of my momma heart not being there to hold her.

Bentli and Demi came to the hospital, and as they arrived in the waiting area, I asked them to come close to me.

Bentli started saying, "Mom, stop! Stop!"

I came out fast and told them what was going on. Bentli started crying and screaming and fell to the floor. Demi fell into the arms of my sister and sobbed. We all cried.

Once I composed myself, and right before they asked to see their dad, I spoke with authority as I mustered all the strength available to me: "There is nothing stopping us. We are fighting this, and with the grace of God, prayers, and chemo, we *are* beating this." I said it with great defiance and conviction.

My emotions were all over the place that day. It is so interesting that the body can go from flight to fight and back to flight so quickly.

I had myself in a great mindset, praying and believing the surgery would come out showing no cancer. When the bomb was dropped, and it was cancer, I felt the warrior come out, but I also felt the sheer panic stirring inside. *How can I do this? How will I manage?*

I refused to allow myself to show panic; it would not help my girls or the situation. I had family members already in panic, which I understood—we had just received a cancer diagnosis. I realized I could sit in my fear and have flight consume me or shove it down and begin the fight.

The one thing I knew was that our God is a good God. Through His healing hands He can work miracles. I knew I would be the rock for my girls. *I had to be.* I would be the shoulder for my husband to cry on, and I would be the warrior that would lead this support group to battle and win!

Doug did well through the night. Every hour they were in to do neurological tests. He was scheduled to have another MRI the following morning, and they were looking at the surgery site to see how his brain was doing.

My family had each other's backs. I am a mama bear when it comes to my girls; mess with them and I might claw your eyes out! We are fighters who battle to the best of our ability! When adversity is thrown at us, we always pull together and plow through it.

As bad as I wanted to ask God why, I decided against doing that. *He is in charge,* I reminded myself regularly. I knew that He had a plan for us, and what that plan was, I had no idea, but I also knew Him as the ultimate healer of all things. I vowed I would turn to Him for guidance and ask Him to hold me on days where my legs were too unsteady to hold me.

I knew I was going to have bad days and cry all day long. I knew I was going to need a lot of help. I realized help would lessen my stress. I have always been good at trying to carry it all on my own, but I also know there are times we need to allow others to assist us. I was reminded that help does not mean I am not capable of doing it. It brought me comfort knowing I had an army standing behind me. We were going to battle and battle until he was healed!

I asked for the healing prayers to keep going strong. I was trusting in the Lord to protect us while we went to battle and to shine His loving presence onto us, for He is in charge and will do me no wrong!

I was expecting miracles.

I was expecting Douglas to be cancer free and for the pathology report to come back as a benign tumor. I expected that the Lord would lay His hands on Doug and perform miraculous healing.

We were told that post-surgery would require a lot of rest for Doug, which would have me running our two businesses. There was a warm welcome to all who volunteered to help us.

The MRI showed that the surgery site looked good and there was no sign of a stroke. We took that as a victory. *Praise Jesus.*

When faced with such a struggle, we work really hard to be warriors, which I embodied for our situation. In the middle of it, I did not know I was showing signs of grief. Denial never *seemed* present during this part of my journey, but as I look now, I can see the denial I expressed. We started a monumental fight, and I was trying to get my new schedule figured out before we were even out of the hospital.

We can be going through hard times in our lives and feel we are in control and not see that grief is starting to sneak in even before a true diagnosis or difficulty shows up. I have come to know this is where I began to experience anticipatory grief, but I had no idea at the time. We can have a warrior mindset and be ready for battle and at the same time feel powerless.

Shock around a diagnosis and the overwhelm of the unknown are very scary, and we need to give space to what we are feeling. The warrior inside doesn't deconstruct from the confusing emotions of sadness and worry we endure in our struggle, and studies have even proven emotions are a lot easier to handle when we can name them. We may not want them, like them, or even want to know them, but when feeling them, it's important we learn what they are so we can feel through them.

Looking back, I can see that this new journey had opened my eyes to what life is truly about, softened my heart to care deeply and sincerely for people in a crisis, and made me realize how well my parents raised me to be a strong person, to never give up, to stand for what I believe in, and to fight when fighting was required! I remember feeling anxious waiting for the reports to come, but we had decided early that it did not matter what we heard, what stage or type, we were committed to fighting it all the same, and with the same outcome intended.

I sat there in the dark, staring out of the hospital window at the cross shining on Table Rock, pondering all the things I could pray about. My heart became calm when I felt in my soul what I needed to pray that night. So, I began…

Thank you, Jesus, for the blessings you have provided me and my family in this time of trials. I ask for your guidance to help me be strong, to give me strength to show to others that through you, all things are possible. Oh God, tonight I give you Doug, my husband and father of my three amazing girls, for I put him in your hands. You, Lord, take your son of Christ and heal him of all sickness, bless him with your spirit, and fill his heart with your love. Oh God, for you are now in control, we are believing in your healing power!

Amen.

Chapter Six

Nice to Be Home!

CaringBridge Entry
March 16, 2014

It is so nice to be home. Doug was released from the hospital yesterday, and he was ready to be home. The continued support takes my breath away. I didn't realize just how many people are here to help us through this unimaginably difficult time.

Today was team pictures for Eagle High softball and there was no way Doug was going to miss it. He loves those girls so much. They have been thrown some big-time adversity—on opening day of the season, their coach was not in the dugout, he was having brain surgery—but they have come together to battle on the field!

Doug speaks to me over and over. "Those girls don't need to worry about me. I need them to battle on the field. You and I, Jack, we'll take care of battling this!"

It is his selflessness trying to protect those young girls from any worry or heartache. He honestly wants them to fight on the field to be the best team possible.

The outpouring of support from all over the valley has been so welcomed. It truly has shown the kindness and care that still is present today. We would not want this any other way. Having the support is comforting because I know I have support from people who will bring me comfort and will sit and listen in my time of need.

Hard things on our journey should never be done alone. We need to rely on loved ones in our lives, giving them opportunities to help us.

There are lots of things going through my mind as I consider and discuss next steps for Doug. All I want is for him to be completely healed and not only survive but thrive.

The final report shows Doug has a glioblastoma high-grade tumor, also known as GBM. He will start chemo and radiation in about a week. We first must allow the incision to heal.

I did not ask any questions.

I do not want to know what GBM high-grade is! It does not matter to me what it is or what stage it is in. We are fighting it no matter what.

Was it the best choice to *not* know what we were facing? I honestly was too scared to know. There, I said it, I was too scared! I decided cancer was cancer and I didn't want to know the severity of Doug's cancer. I feared if I knew the severity of it, I would feel deflated.

I sat and thanked the Lord for the cancer only being in one area. The plan was to focus on that spot with chemo, radiation, positive energies, and the grace of God and His healing ways. We knew we could beat it. If they would have said he had one year or if they would have said ten, we would have tackled this thing with the same process.

God is good. We knew then there were more victories to come!

Chapter Seven

Busy Two Days

Doug decided he wanted to go to the game at Boise High, so we got the pickup parked close enough for him to sit in there and watch it.

Boise High was very sweet and put Doug's initials in chalk behind home plate. At the beginning of the game, they announced that they had Doug in their thoughts and gave him a team picture with the words "Coach Corta Get Well Soon! Lady Braves." What a great bunch of girls. The support was huge and made my heart smile.

During the second inning, Doug felt he needed to be closer to his girls—his team—so with help, he walked to the right field fence. Doug stood there watching until I had to get stern and tell him he had stood long enough and to get back to the pickup. His good friend Ryan went and sat with him so I could be close to the game and cheer.

Ryan said to me after the game, "He is a true coach," and then giggled. I am sure Doug was doing a lot of coaching in the pickup. After the game, Doug walked out to the outfield and spoke to the team. He was so committed to his coaching job and those girls; it was very tough not being out there.

As we were having dinner that evening, the phone rang. I ran over and picked it up.

"Hello?"

An elderly voice answered, "Hi, I'm looking for Mrs. Corta."

"This is me," I replied.

"Hi, this is Mrs. Delaney. I wanted to call you and tell you that my granddaughter had a brain tumor and after finding out she had it, she also found out she was pregnant. Her daughter is now seven years old, and my granddaughter is doing fine. Completely healthy, working really hard, and very strong. I read your sweet story in the paper and felt I needed to call you to give you some positive information."

"Thank you so much for calling me, it truly means a lot to hear this!" This took me by surprise, not only because I didn't know this woman, but also because she took the time to track down my number and made the effort to call. *Who does that these days?*

"Well, honey, you have three girls, and my granddaughter has three girls as well, and she is healed, and I know your sweet husband will be too."

"Oh, Mrs. Delaney, thank you so much."

"Honey, can I ask, does he know the Lord?" She asked with authority and conviction.

"Yes, he does," I eagerly replied, knowing she somehow knew I needed to hear from her.

"Praise God, amen Jesus! He will be healed; you have the faith dear. My granddaughter, I know, was blessed by the healing hands of the Lord. Keep the faith."

We spoke for about twenty minutes; she told me a little about her life and asked if she could call me again. I told her if she felt she needed to call me to please call.

I can now see how God shows himself in so many ways, and when we were going through our own journey, I easily identified those appearances. We found ourselves in melancholy and then situations like this phone call would occur. I saw God show up more and more as we traveled this journey. These appearances always brought me peace and comfort when comfort wasn't being found. This I believe was the Lord working through an Earth angel, one of many. She never called again.

Chapter Eight

Game Plan!

As I sat one night thinking about how I did not want to know anything about Doug's tumor—what it was, what stage it was, anything—I began to look at it as I would coaching. As a basketball coach, I scout the teams I'm going to be playing. I look at what defense I might need to use and what offense I will run against them. I put that together to come up with the best game plan to beat them.

So why am I not scouting this?

Why wasn't I putting together the best game plan to come out and beat this? *Maybe fear.* I know I wanted facts and not all the stuff on the internet that usually leaves a person feeling like there's not a single chance of survival.

I decided I would *get* a scout, but I wouldn't do it myself this time. I wanted a scout that would look at everything and give me only what I needed to hear. So, I asked my cousin, Shanan. She agreed to research and look into treatments, severity of the cancer, and stories of others that may help in our game plan.

I even told her, "Whatever you feel you need to tell me is exactly what I'm supposed to hear. Don't question yourself."

I put my scout in place, and she came up with some great info. Statistics were discovered along with the different types of treatments that have been performed on glioblastoma tumors.

She felt I only needed minimal information at this point, which I was completely okay with. I didn't want to know what the average survival rate was, if there wasn't a cure for this type of cancer, or how aggressive it would be. I didn't want to lose the wind from my sails.

The game plan was being put in order.

We had our post-op visit with Doug's neurosurgeon; it went well. He took out the stitches and said the incision had healed nicely. He told us Doug would start radiation and chemo. He would do another MRI in two months to see if the tumor was growing. He would follow it with an MRI every two months.

He said that if the tumor looked like it was growing back, he would go back in and take more of the tumor out which possibly meant losing some of Doug's left-side movement.

This was a concern of ours since before the first surgery and it caused him a lot of anxiety. We had discussed and decided we would face any outcome head-on, but I could always see his concern about not being able to do everything he has always done. We left it in the hands of the surgeon, and we were praying the tumor would not grow!

It had been a week full of information. I was completely exhausted; I felt like I had taken notes for a college class I didn't want to be in.

I prayed and prayed for the Lord to put the exact doctors in our path, and man, He was good to me.

That day, we went to Mountain State Tumor Institute (MSTI) and met with the medical oncologist. She was amazing! I left feeling very blessed and at ease. I knew we were in good hands.

Here is what the medical oncologist told us: "Doug will take Temozolomide seven days a week during the six weeks of radiation. Following that, he will be put on a twenty-eight-day cycle, five days on the chemo pill and twenty-three days off. That will last between four and six months, depending on how things go. He will have lots of labs done to monitor his CBC and liver. We will also be watching his bone marrow to make sure it does not go down too much. He will be put on Bactrim, an antibiotic, as a precaution."

I guess there is a type of pneumonia he could get. *Bad notetaking right there—can't remember the name.* She said about the third or fourth week he would start to feel fatigue, nothing that would put him on bed rest, but he must listen to his body and rest when needed. She told us this was our first phase; we would see how it went and reevaluate after this phase. She said we would see if this would knock it down. She was very informative.

The following Tuesday, we had Doug fitted for his mask. Doug would wear a thermoplastic mask for each radiation treatment. The radiographer took the plastic material that looked like mesh and softened it by placing it in warm water, then placed it over Doug's face until it reached the table of setting or hardening where it would be locked into place. As it cooled, it hardened in the form of his face. It is what would hold his head in place during radiation, and also had the exact marks on it where the radiation would be directed. It's a sort of fail-safe; everything gets lined up and if he isn't in the exact spot, the machine won't turn on. *Technology.*

Doug was feeling really well. He had been out to practices and games—still on the sideline but close by the dugout. He wasn't yet ready to be in the dugout but was definitely coaching his girls!

The joy those girls brought him is crazy; I know that before all this he might have said they brought him headaches, but now we know that wasn't the girls! He truly cared for them and their success. It made me love him a bit more seeing the love he gave those girls and the way he cared for each of them. What a good guy!

As we were leaving MSTI one day, headed to a softball game, I hurried to use the bathroom. As I sat there, I heard a man's voice, and thought, *Oh no! Did I walk into the men's?* Then I heard a lady say, "Don't leave me." I could see a wheelchair.

The man said, "I will be right out the door."

She responded, "I won't be able to push myself back out."

As I washed my hands, I said out loud, "Would you like me to wait for you?"

She said yes, so I waited. When she was ready, I walked closer to the stall and saw an elderly woman, very small and fragile. I told her to sit down, and I would push her to the sink and out to her husband. She washed her hands, and I helped her out the door. I reached down, squeezed her arm, and told her to have a great day.

She grabbed my hand and said, "Thank you, honey, you are an angel to help me." But looking back, I think she was the angel.

We were running late to Bent's game and were in a hurry, but there was something that made me slow down and asked if she wanted me to wait for her, if she wanted help. When she told me thank you, the look in her eyes was as if she could see my soul. There was something about her that brought me peace. She must have been another earth angel.

This is another example of the new life I was living, pausing to help an elderly woman while knowing I was missing a few innings of my own daughter's softball game. See, the lesson there was to be present in the moment. If I would have been too in my head, I would not have heard the elderly man tell his wife he would be outside the door, and I would not have truly heard or recognized her worry about being unable to push herself out. Pausing in our own journeys can impact others' lives, which in turn enriches ours.

It was a crazy day for me, and I was feeling frazzled. So, I went to my Bible and randomly opened it. This is what I opened to:

Psalms 106:1-3

Praise the Lord. Give thanks to the Lord, for he is good; his love endures forever. Who can proclaim the mighty acts of the Lord or fully declare his praise? Blessed are they who maintain justice, who constantly do what is right.

Through everything we faced, we praised the Lord and gave thanks for every victory. Seeing, recognizing, and acknowledging the littlest victories and giving glory to God for them, I know now is our duty. It is about slowing to see our journey, and those we are meeting, and how our story is touching lives.

Chapter Nine

Added Game Plan

We had a date we were supposed to start Doug's chemo and radiation. We, however, *did not* start that day.

We were guided to a wellness clinic instead. We discovered the clinic from a friend who told me how it helped her mom through her cancer fight. She encouraged us to call them and see how or if they could help Doug.

When we called, they asked if he had started any treatment, which we had not. That was a positive because they wanted to work with a "clean" system—basically, no chemo in him.

We had a visit with them, and they gave us the program Doug would best be suited for. It was a daily dose of numerous supplements, along with a personalized diet that, of course, the girls and I would also follow. Immediately we cut out all sugar and dairy and shifted to reduce red meat (only once a week). These changes were embraced because it would get his body ready to receive chemo. It made sense. We decided to build Doug's body up as strong as we could before starting chemo and radiation. This process took three weeks. After the three weeks, we then began treatment.

I felt the prayers from everywhere. There were moments my knees started to tremble because I was mentally, emotionally, and physically exhausted from trying to hold it together. On my plate, I was managing everything: running the businesses, keeping my household going, navigating support for everyone involved, and just being sad for my husband. During times like those, I was absolutely certain someone was praying for us because the strength was restored to my legs.

I love the Lord and what He can do for all of us. Through Him, all things are possible. This battle would be won. We knew we needed to get the right processes in line to come out fighting as hard as we could.

I had been coaching youth basketball for many years. Basketball was my happy place. This was where I got to mentor young female athletes not just in the game of basketball but in the game of life. It truly brought me joy.

I was coaching my basketball team one year, and at the second practice, I sat the girls down. I told them how talented they all were. I explained how some had strengths where others didn't and those, in turn, had strengths where others didn't, but *together* they were very talented. They were strong. Not just in the sense that they could score points or make a steal; they were talented all the way around.

I looked each of them in the eyes and told them, "I am believing we will be in the championship game at the end of the season, and we will win that game! Now I need each of you to believe it." I paused for a second to let them absorb what I said. I followed up a bit stern: "I need each of you to not just *hope* for it, not just think *maybe*, not just think *that would be cool*. I need you all to *believe it*! The process will be hard, and we will practice like no other, but we will have fun while we do it."

I'm not sure if they thought I was crazy or weird or plain stupid. Or maybe they read into it and truly believed it because my little team lost only one game all season. We made it to the championship game, and we won!

It was hard work—a huge commitment—and a matter of doing our jobs well, but I feel mostly it was *believing*. Believing in themselves, in the process, in the coaches, in the game, and in the power of good. I love those girls so much; they will have a special place in my heart forever.

I share this story because I felt I was at that same place in the cancer journey. I wasn't coaching the girls' basketball team this time but fighting for my husband. I believed. I believed he would be healed. I believed in the power of prayer. I believed in the doctors, and I believed in Christ! I believed in something greater than I can even imagine. I believed we would have a testimony like never before, and I believed we would rejoice in the joy of victory! I believed we would win!

I always prepared for trials along the way, but I knew when I got knocked down, I would stand back up a little bit taller. Through any journey we become better people, better teachers for what is next. I know now how important it is to believe in the processes we face, believe in doctors, believe in the Lord to answer prayers, believe in it all! And most importantly, I continued to believe in the healing power of the Lord.

I know how crazy it is that in the blink of an eye, life is flipped upside down. I could have questioned why we were on this journey, and don't get me wrong, it crossed my mind, but I also realized this journey taught us something. We were taught to slow down and take note of the lessons being handed to us. I'm still learning how slowing down in our busy lives can enable us to gain wisdom in our own story.

I was also learning about strength, a strength I never knew I had.

I was speaking with my girls and was telling them there were lots of lessons to be learned through this process, and a lot of people were being reached. I said maybe by sharing our story, we could inspire one person to look at life a bit differently.

Z looked up at me and said, "Mom, I prayed before. Well, I thought what I was doing was praying, but since this happened to Dad, I pray every day and I pray to the God you speak of."

What a sweet young lady I have. She brought a tear to my eye.

My poor babies, oh what they must have been going through, their little hearts had to be hurting. I prayed for strength for those three beauties and guidance every day. Whenever I asked how they were doing I often got the quick answer of "I'm fine." I am pretty sure they were struggling and processing all of this and protecting me while they acted strong and brave. *They are more like me than I realized.*

Douglas was raised Catholic, and I was not raised in a church. My parents always talked about God, and when my sisters and I were old enough, we could decide where we wanted to go to church. I attended Center Point Church for seven years. I, like my mom, did not push my kids. I invited them to go with me, and I talked about the messages from Sunday service. I knew they were watching.

To hear they were starting to tap into God and find their way into His loving arms brought a lot of joy and lightness to my heart, even under difficult circumstances.

Psalms 84:11-12

> *For the Lord God is a sun and shield; the Lord bestows favor and honor; no good thing does he withhold from those whose walk is blameless. Oh Lord Almighty, blessed is the one who trusts in you.*

Chapter Ten

Let's Be Real, People!

1 Corinthians 16:13

Be on guard, stand firm in the faith; be men of courage; be strong.

Doug and I and our good friend Ryan colored Easter eggs the week before Easter. Doug questioned me when I came home with eggs and dye. I told him I love coloring eggs, and the girls don't want to do it so I'm doing it myself. He was such a trooper and joined in. I think the fact that Ryan came over made it an easier decision.

We laughed until we had tears running down our faces. Who knew coloring Easter eggs would be so dang fun? Sometimes we must find joy in the simplest things, as silly as it was that three grown adults were coloring Easter eggs.

Easter Sunday was amazing! We attended church, and then Doug and I went home to have lunch.

Bentli and Demi went to my aunt's house where all of my family was getting together. When Doug decided to take a nap, I drove over to say hi to everyone.

Man, was that good for my soul to be around those people, even for a short visit. My family is quite fabulous. It was good to see everyone.

Leaving Doug home alone was very hard, and I felt like I should be with him—just in case he needed me or something. I was putting a lot of pressure on myself, but I also knew he was okay for that time. I stayed for a quick visit but with Doug was where I needed to be.

As I was leaving, I began to cry. *What in the world is wrong with you, girl?* I asked myself. *Why are you crying? Is it because you're always the last to leave and this time you were the last to show but the first to leave? Is it because Doug could not go with you? Is it nothing at all?* And I realized as I was questioning myself that I was crying because I was overcome with love. There were no words spoken but I could feel this enormous power of love and support from each one of my family members. It was awesome!

Let's be real, family is so important. They are the ones that, without saying a word, have your back. They love you all the time, give you support in good and in bad, help you at all costs. Family, to me, is a high priority! I love every single one of them! That Sunday was a good day!

————————

CaringBridge Entry
April 21, 2014

Today, Doug's neurosurgeon called and confirmed it is glioblastoma brain cancer—they had sent the pathology slide away for a second opinion. I am feeling like the wind has been taken from my sail and I'm punched in the gut again! We both were thinking, hoping, it would come back with a different result.

CANCER SUCKS! I'm screaming at the top of my lungs, **"CANCER SUCKS!"**

I am feeling weak, a bit anxious. I have had a great talk with myself tonight—beat myself up a bit. (Don't worry, I only gave myself one black eye!)

I pondered for a moment why I set myself up. *Why did I think it would come back any different from what Boise had diagnosed?* I guess it was HOPE! I truly *hoped* for a different diagnosis. I *wanted* a different tumor. I didn't even care if it was a tumor, I'd just hoped for a different one. Glioblastoma *is* the worst of the worst!

I sat with tears running down my face, questioning, *why am I being so weak?* But was I truly weak? No, I was feeling the absolute fear that Douglas had stage four brain cancer. The potential reality of it all had shown its face. It was my warrior self that wanted—or maybe thought I needed—to be strong for everyone else. Again, I was pushing my feelings down when they came up. This was a moment I needed to give myself grace. I needed to be okay with sitting in my sadness and realize what I was feeling was a normal step through this. Grief was happening, but I was not seeing how much it was a part of my life yet. I didn't acknowledge it. I refused to name it.

"Be strong girlfriend," I tell myself aloud as I look in the mirror. "Pull it together, you need to be strong!"

I seriously hate when that Jacki talks to me. She needs to back off. Tonight, I want to be weak, I want to cry, I want to scream at the top of my lungs. Just let me throw a fit like a two-year-old who isn't getting her way.

Emotions have intentionally been set aside, pushed away, shoved to the pit of all pits. The fear of the unknown has been weighing on me, along with the anger that wants to boil out from the hand we have been dealt. I am consciously feeling it. Tonight, I don't want to be strong; tonight, I can't hold myself up! Tonight, I WANT TO BE SAD!

Chapter Eleven

Big-Time Prayers, Please

Romans 12:12

Be joyful in hope, patient in affliction, faithful in prayer.

CaringBridge Entry
April 22, 2014

I did not get much sleep last night. I finally closed my eyes at 2:45 a.m., and my alarm went off at 6:00.

A racing mind is the worst, and I simply could not shut it off. I was going through all aspects of this new journey. So, I prayed...

Oh, Lord Almighty, give me the peace I am forever needing at this moment. Hold me, Lord, and comfort me as I feel weak tonight. Pour your love onto me and my heart, and reassure me you, Lord, are in control, you have the power to do all miraculous things.

I am asking tonight, as I am feeling no strength in my legs to hold myself up, that you will shine, shine through me Lord. Through this trial, I know lessons are being learned, seeds are being planted in those who need you. I trust you will use me, this journey, and our faith to help one person. You, Lord, will not fail me. Tonight, my soul cries, and it is you that answers those cries.

Bless my amazing husband, the father of my three beauties, that he will be healed by the grace of God, he will be healed! You Lord will show the victories to all of us.

Amen.

Tomorrow afternoon, Doug is scheduled for an MRI. This is where I'm asking for big prayers! We are praying the tumor has not grown. Since we put off treatment to work on getting Doug's body strong enough to handle chemo, they want to check to see if the tumor has grown. Once we get the results of the MRI, we will then most likely start the chemo and radiation.

Doug is feeling really strong. He has tons of energy and is doing really well. We both feel we made the right decision by going to the wellness clinic before chemotherapy; we have heard how devastating it can be on even the healthiest of people. We will continue with the wellness clinic through the whole process; they are now family.

Tonight, I am asking this army that stands by me for one more prayer for Doug.

May we rejoice tomorrow or the next with a victory won. No growth of the tumor!

Psalms 71:14

But as for me, I will always have hope; I will praise you more and more.

Chapter Twelve

Results Are In

CaringBridge Entry
April 24, 2014

The ringing of my phone has me instantly looking at the screen to see who is calling. My heart starts beating a bit faster when the neurosurgeon's name appears.

"Hello?" I answer.

"Is Jacki there?" came the masculine voice of the surgeon from the receiver.

"This is me." I am suddenly frozen and eager to hear the news.

He asks, as if it were a friendly, daily interaction, "How are you?"

"I am well, thanks." *I am not well.* I am terrified, petrified, overwhelmed, and confused among a dozen other feelings, but as if to spare the doctor, my answer stays simple.

"How is Doug feeling?" he asks, prolonging the inevitable.

"He is doing pretty good, thanks for asking." I was being cordial, but I really wanted to scream TELL ME THE RESULTS!

"We got the results back on the MRI. It shows slight growth of the tumor." His announcement is promptly followed by a void, a pause, an emptiness on the other end.

It takes me a second to respond as the news was not what we wanted to hear. "Umm, okay."

"I know this isn't what we wanted, but it is very small growth."

The surgeon goes on to explain that he wants to see how the tumor reacts to radiation and chemo. If it does not react well to the radiation and chemo, he would like to do another surgery to remove more of it. His concern as mentioned before is that Doug might lose some of his left-side movement if the surgery happens. However, he made it clear that leaving the tumor is not the answer as long as it is operable.

We start radiation and chemo on Monday morning!

It has been a very rough day for the both of us. We are grateful we have gotten his body to a very strong point. We are believing he will fly through this next phase with little to no complications. *Is this my way of coping with the news? Or is it me truly believing he will fly through this because we have worked so hard to build his strength?* This is where my faith is holding strong.

We are continuing to use the wellness clinic along with radiation and chemo. They have helped us so much already. The doctors have told us that when the tumor is dying, it might show on the MRI that it has grown. But what it does is swells before it dies, appearing as potential growth. Since we started working with the wellness clinic to get Doug on a strict diet and supplement regimen building strength in his body, there is a part of me that hopes this is what is happening. It is swelling before it dies!

I will be honest; I have cried a lot today and I have felt very weak. I have shut everyone out. I did not feel like talking to *anyone*! I only wanted to be with my husband.

Now that we have his body strong, we are going to battle! We believe in Christ that his body will stay strong through the radiation and chemo, and Doug WILL be healed!

The Lord has a plan, and we will see what He has for us. In this moment, I truly believe His plan is to have the treatment and the tumor will no longer grow. I also think it is my way of coping. My faith is not in question, but in moments of doubt and being scared, I use my faith to cover up all of that. There is no distrust; it is my way of portraying strength when I am feeling weak.

Proverbs 3:5-6

Trust in the Lord with all your heart and lean not on your own understanding; in all your ways acknowledge him, and he will make your paths straight.

The unknown in our journey is always a battle. Right now, while Doug is physically fighting cancer, we are both waging a mental battle to overcome the uncertainty we're feeling.

How will he take radiation? How will his body react to chemo? Will he be sick? Will he be tired?

Whenever I think of chemotherapy treatment, I envision an IV with a bag of fluid dripping into a tube that feeds into the arm. There was a relief when we were told Doug would take a chemo pill. No IV. No long hours of sitting in a cold hospital room waiting for a slow-flowing bag to empty. The anxiousness that stirs up sitting there would not happen. We would be here at home. There would be a glass of water grabbed and one pill swallowed. That's it.

The harsh reality of the potency of the pill was evident when we were told that no one else can touch the chemo pills—only Doug. The seriousness of the treatment was hitting him. *No one can touch it, but he can put it in his body? Seriously?* That says a lot about what we are stepping into.

We are going at this with a fight. There is no backing down; we are prepared and strong. I am believing in radiation and chemo, but I am believing even more in the power of prayer and the healing hands of the Lord.

Philippians 4:13

I can do everything through Him who gives me strength.

Chapter Thirteen

Radiation Number One... DONE!

Oh my gosh, I was not prepared for the emotions I would be going through sitting there before, while, and after my sweet Doug was being zapped by a machine.

We sat in the waiting room—a smaller waiting area away from the main waiting area. *Swamp People* was on the TV. I am now thinking it was set on that to keep my mind off what we were doing there. It is a very interesting show, to say the least, and it seems like it was an intentional distraction for everyone.

A sweet lady sat in the waiting area with us, knitting. As we watched this goofy show, she said to us, "That is a huge swamp; it takes over an hour to get across it on the bridge that goes over it."

I said to her, "That is big."

She smiled so sweetly at me. There was a calmness about her that made me feel it too.

The tech came to get Doug, but as I stood, she said, "Oh, today, you can stay here; this first time, we will take only Doug but another time you can come back."

Her response instantly put me on the defense. I felt I needed to be there with Doug. Doug and I had talked about praying over the room and mask where he would get treatment. I looked at her and said, "Okay, but I would like to pray over his mask before his first treatment."

She told me to follow them. She took Doug into her room to go over some things and pointed to a room across the hall and told me to go in.

I walked into the cool treatment room, and there was a huge machine and a table off to one side of it. The mask was near where Doug would be lying. Another tech was standing with her back to me. She turned and seemed surprised to see me. She joked that I didn't fit the description that she'd been given of Doug. I told her I wanted to pray over his mask. I asked her if I could hold it or if I needed to leave it where it was.

She said, "You can hold it, my dear."

I placed the mask in my hands, I had it close to my body, and for a moment I held it. I wanted to feel every part of it. Then, I began to pray, and as I prayed, tears started running down my face.

I returned to the waiting area, anxious to visit with the sweet lady that had been there earlier. She was nowhere to be found. She had packed up all her knitting, drinks, snacks, everything—*where did she go?* I guess she had done her job; she had brought me calmness when I needed it.

I sat in the waiting area alone while not completely alone. I had my thoughts, my angels, and someone with their arms wrapped around me! Maybe Grammy, maybe it was her holding me for a moment, knowing what was coming next.

Doug walked back into the waiting area, crying!

He sat down next to me. I put my arm on his back as he tried to not cry.

I leaned in and whispered in his ear, "Do you want to talk about it?"

He shook his head no.

"It's okay to cry. It is okay to be scared. Know we are in this together, and I LOVE YOU!" I sat there massaging his back. I love how the Lord helps us to be strong when others need us. In truth, all I wanted to do was crumble when I saw the tears.

We went in to see the doctor. She looked at Doug and asked how he was doing. It got silent; he began to cry. We all sat there and allowed him to cry.

I put my arm around him, as he looked up with the big old alligator tears and said to her, "I have never been scared like this!"

The lump in my throat grew very large, as the doctor said to him, "How human you are."

Wow, I loved that! She said four words, four words that were *huge*. She went through how things were going to go, the radiation treatment, and the labs to be monitored along with the chemo. She made clear there would be strong communication between her and the medical oncologist. She asked about our treatments with the wellness clinic.

I was feeling so blessed that we had both the wellness clinic doctors and our medical doctors on our team.

As she stood to leave, she looked at Douglas and said, "Let's kick this thing's ass!"

That night, he would take his first chemo pill, and it took some time for it to go down.

After the treatment, I went to the salon to work. I had no idea that day would be so emotional. I had to go to the salon and talk about it all day. *What was I thinking?*

The day went better than I thought. All my clients were amazing. I guess that's why they are mine. Everyone asked how things were and then we visited.

My first client of the day was exactly who I needed. She talked about her senior daughter and her plans for the future; we talked about Z being at college and how she was coming home for the summer. We chatted all through her appointment, and when we finished, she asked how things were going.

I told her fine. *Fine* was an easy answer for me. It was my go-to when I did not want to go into detail about how I was truly feeling. I felt like I was protecting those who were asking. *Why do I do that?* It was like if I went into detail about how I was feeling, it would possibly make them sad, and I did not want any more sadness. Looking back now, I see that I actually took from them the opportunity to support me and console me.

There is a fine line between saving others the heartache I am feeling and removing opportunities to gain support and consolation through difficulty. It's easy to provide such things from behind the salon chair, but role reversals with my clients and friends made me feel like I was burdening them.

That day, that special client kept my emotions down by being herself and visiting with me like she always does. The normalcy was a blessing. Her actions, without even knowing what she was doing, gave me added strength to get me through the day.

My life is a blessing. This journey I have chosen is a rough one, but I know I will travel this it with amazing people by my side and a God that will not fail me!

Chapter Fourteen

Week One under Our Belt

CaringBridge Entry
April 30, 2014

It has been an exhausting week for both Doug and me. Going every day to radiation and oncologist appointments, working, and then to our girls' activities have been a bit much.

Doug has done really well this first week. After his first radiation treatment, he did have some pressure in his head, which is normal because it can cause some swelling.

We are looking forward to having the weekend off with no chemo or radiation. Maybe some rest, *oh wait...* Bentli starts district softball tomorrow and Demi has three basketball games and a softball tournament in Fruitland, so I guess the only place we'll be resting is in the car!

I'm trying to keep our life as normal as it can be with a cancer diagnosis. Not only for Doug but for our girls as well. When I notice that Doug is getting run down and tired, I do my best to have him rest, but he isn't having it. He wants to be at all the girls' activities as if nothing is wrong.

We have five more weeks of leaving the house at 7:30 a.m. to travel twenty-five minutes one direction to the hospital for Doug to receive his radiation treatment. I do my best to help keep his anxiety under control and mine in check while he's also taking his chemo pill each day, Monday through Friday. I'm feeling very blessed that this first week went so well.

Through our God, all things are possible, even when we are feeling a bit weak and overwhelmed or overextended. I know He is guiding me and loving me. I believe He is using me for something greater. I am trusting in Him to do me no wrong. His plan for us is grander than I can imagine or see. Trusting and holding onto my faith in this journey is what will get me through. It is believing that God is in control of this and knowing everything He is doing is in line with His plan for our lives.

It does not mean I will understand or actually see what He is doing in the moment, but what I know is the foundation my faith is built on has trust in it.

Chapter Fifteen

Week Two

CaringBridge Entry
April 31, 2014

We started week two off with a bang. Yesterday, the best part of the day was Z—our eldest daughter—got home from college for the summer! It's exactly what this mom needs: all three girls under my roof for a bit. Doug is so excited to have her home.

We are starting to see some side effects of the radiation and chemo. Doug is having a hard time remembering little things. It's not super noticeable but being with him twenty-four seven, I am seeing it. He even spoke tonight and said, "If I interrupt you, it's because I need to speak. If I wait, I can't remember what I was going to say!"

I told him I understood, and interruptions were fine. I can feel a bit of frustration is starting to set in with him.

I could not be prouder of the man I'm doing life with. He has been a champ through all of this so far. I know he's getting sick of my babying him and reminding him to drink his energy drinks, eat food, take his supplements, eat, eat, eat, rest, rest, and rest. I hope one day he will realize I am so persistent because I love him so dang much!

In this stage of our lives, I am being called to truly practice our wedding vows. Doug is a good patient for the most part and "in sickness and in health" is being taken literally around here. I would have the sickness in another way but taking care of my husband is exactly right.

Psalms 71:20

Though you have made me see troubles, many and bitter, you will restore my life again; from the depths of the earth you will again bring me up.

Chapter Sixteen

Long Week Three

We started week three of chemo and radiation. The girls went with us to radiation and the doctors' appointments as they were very interested in seeing for themselves what Dad's protocols were, especially since they are so busy themselves.

They got to see the radiation room. We walked down a long hallway and turned into a large, cold room with this ginormous machine and table.

The stillness that followed us into the room had me wondering if tears were about to begin. The tech was very informative for the girls and prepared them to see him get locked into his mask.

He sat on the edge of the table and slowly lay on his back. The techs walked over with Doug's mask and began placing it over Doug's face and head.

I had apprehension that this may be too much for my girls. With a quick glance I witnessed three strong young girls standing, eyes locked on their dad. With a few turns of the locks on the mask, Doug was in position on the table. We stepped out of the room and into a smaller room where the radiologist performed the radiation with the clicks of a button.

We only stayed for a split second and went back to the waiting area to wait for Doug to finish. The silence felt heavy as we waited. I asked if they had any questions and almost in unison they said, "No!"

Once with the oncologist, she did her routine check of Doug and then looked at the girls and asked them if they had any questions or concerns. They looked back and forth to each other, and I jumped in and said it is okay, urging them to answer. One by one we got, "No, I'm good, no."

I think it was good for the girls to see where we go every morning and meet the doctors taking care of their dad.

Doug had done really well that week with his radiation and chemo. I thanked God every night for blessing him with good health and strength. I am thankful he had so much energy to keep going to practices and games with his team. I'm grateful he was able to take Z out to do some front tosses to work on her swing, along with traveling to watch Demi play softball. I was so glad he continued to do the things he loved.

I truly believed his not working helped keep his stress levels down so he could focus on healing. It was extra work for me, but that was also my season to take care of him and everything else, which included things that came up with the girls.

I didn't know why I was meant to shoulder all of this. I found myself mired in the tasks at hand, which might have been a blessing in disguise. I wasn't forced to wallow with nothing to do. I had *plenty* to do, and it never seemed to end.

Luckily, I was not at my breaking point when Demi said her back hurt. I chalked it up to her being sore from sports. To be sure, I decided to take her to the doctor, and as the doctor was feeling the area, she took a deep breath and said, "I believe it is a soft tissue mass and we need to get on top of this."

My heart sank and screamed in my head, *What is going on?* This was certainly pushing me close to breaking. First my husband and then my baby. *What's next?*

We were waiting for blood work when I got a call that Demi was scheduled for an ultrasound in thirty minutes.

At that point, a bit of panic set in. Her doctor called that evening to say the blood work was normal, but the X-ray showed a curvature in her spine, and she ordered an MRI and an appointment with an orthopedic doctor.

By then, anger had filled me, and I was feeling deflated. I was dealing with Doug's fight and figuring out life with cancer, trying to run two businesses, and keeping my girls uplifted, and then this… *why?*

Yep, I was frustrated.

I asked, *why, why so much, why now, why me, why Demi… why?*

I sat by myself in the front room in silence. Hearing my own thoughts, I spoke, "Oh Lord, you are doing a good job piling my plate very high these days, but do not worry because I am a fighter, and I will not back down!"

The results of Demi's MRI showed she had a stress fracture of her lower lumbar area, L5. They said this was common with teenagers who play high impact sports. She was limited to walking for three weeks with no heavy lifting. She had to start physical therapy and slowly bring back activities to see how it felt. She added jogging, side-to-side movement, running, lifting weights, and then she was released to full activities.

Demi was feeling very discouraged not being able to do anything. She showed signs of relief in us finally knowing what was wrong.

That had been my long week three, but on a positive note… Doug was halfway through treatment!

Psalms 31:24 ·

Be strong and take heart, all you who hope in the Lord.

———————

I was not raised in the church, but my family believed in God. There was a Bible in the house, which must mean something, right? I've known of a higher power for quite a long time, but did I have a relationship with it? A true relationship? Nope, not me. I said my prayers every night, wasn't that enough?

When someone asked if I believed in God, I always answered yes. For years, that is all I had. I think that is all I thought I needed. Someone asked me what religion I was, and I would say, "Christian." I believed in the Lord, and I figured saying Christian was all I needed.

My relationship with the Lord grew stronger with the birth of my third daughter. She was born with her stomach not connected to her esophagus, which is a whole other story. But I witnessed prayers for my baby being answered.

Two years after her birth, my dad had a tremendous accident, and prayers were said for him immediately. The doctors told us with his brain injury, he had a 1 percent chance to live… 1 percent! Tell me prayers don't get answered.

Those were two huge things in my life which helped build my relationship with the Lord, but there were small things that the Lord had also played out in my life. Evidence showed up in many places, from an unplanned bill with no funds to pay it and an unexpected refund from another company sent due to overpayment, to hitting every red light and coming up on an accident that just happened. Those were the things I didn't understand right in that moment, but God is good and sees it work out.

Five months before Doug was diagnosed with cancer, I was let go from a job I enjoyed. I was confused and had no understanding of it. I later saw the Lord was clearing my schedule, knowing what was coming. At the time, I only saw the downside of being let go, and I couldn't see that good would come from it. I remember thinking that with every door shut a new one would open. I didn't understand if we didn't want that door to shut, then how could something better come? Well, that comes from trusting the Lord.

In moments that we feel are full of negatives, we need to trust and seek out the positives in them. There had been such a shift in how Doug, the girls, and I began approaching life. We began to see more of the good in people. We were giving more grace to areas we may not have given it before this. Life seemed fuller since the diagnosis.

I was facing one of the scariest things I had ever faced. But I had a peace about me. I believe it was because I had a relationship with Christ. I had allowed Him into my heart. I didn't just say my prayers at night, I read the Word, I tried my best to practice His Word, and I shared with others how life can change with Him in it.

Having had this relationship only established a deeper trust. It showed me what could happen when I hung onto the slightest bit of hope. This relationship only added an enhanced strength within me—a strength only He can provide. Now, I turn all things to Him and release my attempt at control so He may use His power, either on His own or through me! Gaining this relationship changed my outlook on all things, and the importance of it only justified the journey we were on.

There are still times that I crumble and become weak, and that is okay because I know God will be my strength. Remember our God is a good God. He is the ultimate healer and through Him all things are possible!

Finding ourselves relying on family and friends to support us proved the hand of God existed in all of it. Their loving support brought so much comfort to all of us.

Observing my girls' friends step up to show support and love strengthened my belief in the power of friendships. Experiencing it with my own friends and dear family showed how good our God is.

Nothing is more superior than the love of Jesus. He surpasses everyone! And He shines through so many.

Chapter Seventeen

So Many Appointments

CaringBridge Entry
May 20, 2014

It was another busy week full of doctors' appointments.

Tuesday was Doug's last radiation treatment! Man, where did six weeks go?

They will wait another six weeks after the last treatment to do an MRI because radiation can cause swelling. This will be his baseline MRI to gauge our starting point of the size of the tumor, and we are hoping to see the treatment has been working. Then, three months from that, they will do another MRI and then compare the two. Meanwhile, he will be off chemo for twenty-three days, then on it for five straight days, then off for twenty-three days and on it for five days. This will continue for up to twelve months. We will continue to see the doctors at the wellness clinic to keep Doug's internal body strong.

Doug was feeling frustrated with the fact we will not really know anything until October. I told him we must just keep believing everything we're doing is working. Maybe that's easier said than done. He was getting tired of the same routine every day. The monotony of the day was what was so tiresome. Routine is good when you have flexibility, but there was no flexibility in Doug's schedule.

To change things up, I recommended he go with Z and Demi to Pascoe, Washington for Demi's softball tournament.

Their trip was hard for me, I guess because Doug and I have been together twenty-four seven since the diagnosis. I really should have been sick of him, but I missed him. I called to see where he was and to tell him I missed him.

His response to me was, "Jack, we are only an hour from the house!"

He had been my constant; Doug had been with or near me for many months. In the quiet of not having to be on duty, I actually sat, and no one needed me, which caused some of what I was feeling. Plus, I worried: *Would he be okay without me?*

I ran some errands, feeling weary and weepy. As I walked through the store, I went around the corner into an aisle full of dishes, and right there, when you think He's not listening, He throws it right back in your face. The aisle was full of dishes that all had the words from Proverbs 3:5: "Trust in the Lord with all of your heart."

The loneliness of Doug being gone had me curled up in his chair pondering what I was feeling. The time alone, in the silence, brought forth the bubbling of emotions and thoughts. Allowing tears to flow I quickly found myself at the end of an empty box of tissues. My mind wandered from thoughts of *is Doug okay without me on this trip?* to, *am I advocating for everything that Doug needs for his treatment?* Then of course there were thoughts emerging that I instantaneously pushed back down. I couldn't face them right then; they would have to be dealt with another day. And as if the Lord whispered in my ear, I heard *you may rest.*

2 Thessalonians 3:16

Now may the Lord of peace himself give you peace at all times and in every way. The Lord be with all of you.

Chapter Eighteen

Is This Normal?

As we drove to radiation one morning, I asked Doug how he was feeling about it being his last radiation.

"Fine, I guess," was his answer.

We both couldn't believe how fast six weeks went by. The more we talked, the more I could feel myself starting to be filled with anxiety, maybe even a few tears were building. Unsure of where this was coming from, I began giving myself a pep talk in my head.

Keep it together, Jack! He is doing well, so you need to hold it together!

We walked into Mountain State Tumor Institute and saw all the same faces we'd seen for the last six weeks. Some stories we knew, others we didn't, but we recognized their faces. It's crazy how connected we had begun to feel to each of them.

As always, we were greeted by the sweet receptionist we saw every morning, always with a beautiful smile on her face. "Congrats Doug, it is your last treatment!"

How nice that sounded, but at the same time, how scary it sounded to me—*why is it scary? Why am I not jumping for joy?* I had been warned that Doug might have mixed emotions about the last treatment. I was told he might be sad. But no one mentioned that I might also be sad.

Well, he was a champ. Today, it was his wimpy wife that struggled. I'm not sure why or what was even causing it. All I knew was that I was a bundle of nerves and wanted to cry and be pissed all at the same time.

Doug went back for this last treatment. The tech came out and put his arm around Doug and said, "Last one, let's do this!"

As I sat there alone, I was waiting for an amazing young mom I met two weeks ago. She was fighting breast cancer with two children at home. She came down for radiation during the week.

Please hurry and get here, I thought. I wanted to tell her it had been so nice visiting with her every morning. I wanted to thank her for sharing her tender story with me and to wish her well. But unfortunately, Doug was done before she came in.

Wait… My husband is done. D. O. N. E. And I am sad I didn't get to see the young mom one last time. *I should be jumping for joy, right?* I should jump for joy.

I think the sadness came from a few things. But one thought that really hit me is how I would never know how the other patients' stories ended. We became bonded with these people without even really knowing them very well. I am praying that someday our paths will cross, and I'll be able to see how their stories ended. I am praying for complete healing and long, vibrant, healthy lives for everyone.

We walked out of St. Luke's, holding hands like we always did. As we walked out, I could feel a tighter squeeze on my hand. Was he feeling anxious, was he sad, was he scared, was I looking into it too much?

I asked, "Can you believe we are done?"

He responded, "Nope!"

Oh great, one-word answer. He must be having a hard time, he must be scared, he must... Oh, my word, Jack, pull it together!

As we drove home, Doug said that it would be nice not driving down this road every morning.

I replied, "Yes, it will."

The drive home was a bit quieter than normal, *should I question it or leave it?* I tried to make small talk. *What in the world, we have been married for twenty-one years and I'm making small talk? I'm talking about the stupid stuff people talk about on first dates.*

It finally hit me. Doug was doing fine... I was *not* doing fine!

I dropped him off at home, and I headed to basketball practice with the young girls I was coaching.

My dear, sweet friend, who I coach with, was there. She said to me, "What are you doing here? I thought there would be a celebration lunch or something."

I smiled and said, "No, not today," as I walked closer.

She said, "How is he doing?"

"Good."

"How are *you* doing?"

Crap.

Why is it when a friend asks things like that you can't hold it together? I began to feel tears and did not want to walk into practice a bawling mess, so I walked off to take a few deep breaths and returned to her.

She also had tears in her eyes. She said, "Is it the thought that his treatment is over? Not knowing and wondering if it even worked?"

Bam!!! She hit the reason for the feelings of the day; I wasn't even aware until she said it to me. *Wondering if it worked!* That was it. My concern about whether Doug was anxious, scared, sad, or nervous wasn't him at all. It was me. I was anxious... I was sad... I was scared!

Tears dampened my cheeks as I kept playing the words over and over in my head. *Did it even work?* It was the unknown that disrupted my thinking which initiated a spiraling effect in my thought process. With a grab of my hand and tears in her eyes, she added, "It is normal to wonder and be scared. You do not have to be strong all the time."

I was so absorbed with my faith and trusting God's plan, that when she said, "Did it even work?" it caused me to question. *Did God do me good? Was His promise what I had wanted?*

We can fall into this at any moment in our journeys, it is called being human. This is the time we must give ourselves grace for real thoughts that come across our minds.

"Thank you! I just didn't realize how having the last radiation treatment would affect me," I told her. We walked into practice where I was able to mentor those amazing young girls. Crazy how assistant coaches do their jobs. They don't even know they are helping a girl out!

I truly believed the Lord had a plan. Through me, He was helping others to find Him, get to know Him, or rekindle a relationship with Him. My prayers were for complete healing of my amazing husband and the father of my children, but it also included prayers for my story to touch the lives of many, to have witnesses of the miracles that can come from the power of prayer.

Chapter Nineteen

Game Plan Has Changed

The wellness clinic that had been helping Doug along the way did not feel his body had recovered enough from the six weeks of chemo and radiation. They were concerned that with the higher doses of chemo coming, his body would not handle it well. They did some testing and encouraged us to wait, hoping to get his kidneys and liver cleared and strong. They had been testing his kidneys and liver throughout this whole process and felt they had been overworked. Of course, there was also a risk to waiting—the tumor could grow.

They told us we ultimately had the final say and they would support us and be by our side no matter what we decided.

Those were the moments I wished I was still a little girl and could cry for my mommy and have her make my decisions for me. But I'm all grown up and we had to do this on our own. And then, I heard in my head, *I am with you to guide you and love you!*

Oh yeah, we were *not* alone. We knew that God was with us!

As we drove home, Doug said, "Jack, I have questioned why I have to take the chemo five days out of the month."

I could feel he was starting to doubt. Doug grew up in a Catholic family but had pulled away from going to church in his adolescent years. He still had his faith; it had just weakened.

I responded, "You need to sit in silence, listen, and pray. But make sure you truly listen for your answer." He looked at me funny, and I continued, "Douglas, I have never pushed church, pushed prayer, or God. I can tell you I believe He can heal all things. That is, if you turn your burdens to Him. He will bless you."

Doug sat there listening attentively, so I kept speaking to him. "You must have the faith. We must *believe* it works out… not hope. We cannot be fearful; you need to allow the Lord in your heart and allow Him to guide you on your decision and see Him work his miracles." I paused for a moment, grabbed his hand, and softly spoke, "Have the faith, my love, for I feel His presence with us. Your answer might come today, or it might be in a few days. Make sure you are aware."

I went to work in the salon, and as I came into the house, Doug announced that he wanted to have the MRI before starting the chemo. I did not question him. Did he sit in silence? Did he pray? Did he decide? I don't know. All I know is there was a peacefulness about him.

My prayers changed day-to-day and that day, I prayed for God Almighty to wrap Doug in His hands and give Doug all the things to help him feel or see the guidance our God has for him. I prayed for Doug's heart to be softened and his strength to be fortified.

Chapter Twenty

MRI

As we walked into St. Luke's, he grabbed my hand. *Oh, how I truly love holding his hand.* He grasped it tighter.

I asked if he was okay as he wiped his eyes. Tears were building; I allowed him to be. I think sometimes we can push; we can say things will be good, we can say "this sucks," we can push to comfort, and in reality, we need to BE! Just sitting with what is in front of us and not taking action, not trying to resolve or find a solution but truly being present in the stillness that surrounds us is hard and full of emotions. It also can be very therapeutic for our souls. So that is what I did.

We checked in, they started an IV for contrast, and we waited in the waiting area. When the tech came to get him, he leaned in and looked me straight in the eyes, gave me a kiss, and said, "Love you!"

I came to a standstill and reevaluated where I was on the journey. Was I going through the motions or was I taking in every moment given to me? Was the journey taking *from* me or was I letting it fill me with growth?

That day was a reminder of the importance of us all being true to ourselves, seriously looking at the life we all are living, and appreciating it. We need to look ourselves in the mirror and ask ourselves: Do we love that person we see? Do we love how we are living our lives? Do we love how we are treating others? Do we love how we are carrying ourselves?

I had to answer those questions honestly for my own peace of mind. I was not sure if I truly loved the girl I saw in the mirror, probably because I had gained some weight and was full of doubt in how I was traveling this journey. I knew I loved how I was living my life because I was living it for my husband and girls. I was giving to them as much as I could and more.

But I learned during that time how to treat others. And it did take some work. Seeing how short life could be will make a person reevaluate the way to react to others and can reveal the simple things that seem maddening. I now choose to see the good in others even when they radiate negative energy. I hold onto how I was raised, and the role model my dad was to me. Never once did I hear him say a bad thing about anyone.

I learned to be true to myself, to be true to others, and to be true in every aspect of my being!

My heart is full of the love I have for Christ, and the love I have for every single person I touch in my journey!

———————

With the baseline MRI complete, we would have another one done in two to three months and compare the tumor.

As I sat in church on Sunday, the pastor talked about being steadfast—staying firm in belief and fixed in place.

I have said before, I believe in the miracles of the Lord, and by the grace of God, I vowed Doug would be healed. I was trusting in the Lord to take my husband in His loving hands and clear his body of sickness. I was screaming from the tops of my lungs: VICTORIES

WILL BE WON! I would *not* allow evil to distract me on my mission with Douglas.

I believed I had the responsibility to keep us on track, to be the warrior in this situation. When others were weak, I stayed in the fight. Had I taken on more pressure than what I needed? Probably, but that is where I wanted to be. I WAS STEADFAST WITH MY FAITH!

Ephesians 6:13-15

> *Therefore put on the full armor of God, so that when the day of evil comes, you may be able to stand your ground, and after you have done everything, to stand. Stand firm then, with the belt of truth buckled around your waist, with the breastplate of righteousness in place, and with your feet fitted with the readiness that comes from the gospel of peace.*

I warned all the evil that might try to come and all the distractions that might try to appear, that they were messing with the wrong girl. I was leading the fight and fighting not only for my husband but also for my family. And because I was so vocal with my faith and my trust in the Lord, I *knew* the enemy would try to take me out. That is why I said, *you are messing with the wrong girl.* Not for selfish reasons, but because I was in the lead.

My faith was stronger than it had ever been, my love for the Lord was tight, and I shared a testimony that kept growing with each day.

I would be lying if I said there were no hard days. My momma heart hurt watching my girls go through that. When I asked how they were doing, I almost automatically got, "Fine." I am pretty sure this was their way of protecting me.

Moments of being scared had been present and that was when the warrior in me took to the forefront and consoled them, reiterating that it was okay to be scared and unsure of what was going to happen. I also reminded them that Dad was strong, and we were fighting this disease with everything we had.

Each day we were living this, I was watching the girls grow up so quickly. The love they showed for their dad was incredible and witnessing all he went through was arduous.

I continued to pray for the next MRI to give us hope that all things were healing, that my best friend and the father of my three beautiful girls would walk beside us on the rest of our journey, healthy and strong. I prayed that all the doors of despair be slammed shut!

I could see where the girls had moments of showing me sadness and being so scared. There were many times they displayed a bravery that I could not believe. This is most likely in conjunction with what I was giving them. I was exhibiting strength and a brave face in protection for them while explaining to them it was okay to be weak, to cry, and to be angry. These were all the *right* things to feel as they watched their dad go through this.

There was something to being reminded that emotions and vulnerability are not weaknesses. I was teaching and encouraging my girls to exhibit strength in ways I wasn't sure I even recognized in myself, but I was showcasing it for them each day.

Chapter Twenty-one

Game Plan Is Taking Us to Seattle!

As we walked into our oncologist appointment there was a heaviness I could feel between Doug and me.

She walked in and said, "How are you guys?"

Almost in unison we responded, "Good."

"We have the results of the MRI, and it looks like the tumor is not responding to treatment."

We sat in defeat, half hearing as she continued, "We need to get you a second opinion out of state. What we have offered here is all we can do, and if we don't get you some other treatment, we are looking at a couple weeks."

I quickly turned from staring at Doug to looking at her with concern. I could have screamed, *what are you talking about two weeks?* but she continued. "This is a vicious tumor, and if we don't get you in to see another specialist, it could mean you have two weeks left."

Doug became very scared; he stood up quickly and began to pace. I spoke up, "We are good, Douglas, we are good."

He began to cry.

I then asked, "What do we need to do to get into a specialist?"

"I have my nurse working on it now, we are trying two locations to get you in, one is in San Francisco and the other is in Seattle. I am sorry to give you the news."

Doug headed toward the door to leave as I grabbed his arm to slow him. "Will I hear from the nurse?"

"Yes, she will call you as soon as she has an appointment."

As we walked out the door, I softly told her, "Thank you."

Once we were out of the office, I could feel the fear in Doug. He wanted to get out of the hospital and was trying to find the nearest exit. We found ourselves under a small tree in the back of the hospital.

"What is going on, Jack? Why, why, *why* is this happening?" Tears fell.

I had nothing; all I said was, "I think we call our pastor and have him come."

Within fifteen minutes, we stood with our pastor under that small tree. I shared with him the news we had just gotten along with the concerns Doug was experiencing. He began to pray over Doug, over our family, and for guidance on the best place we were to be for this next step of treatment.

We spent about one and a half hours with him outside of the hospital. He brought what we needed. We could feel the presence of God standing firm with us.

My heart felt like we needed to be in Seattle. I could not understand why I had such a knowing about that. Was it because Seattle was closer to us? I just recall a strong pull in my spirit that was where we needed to go.

When the nurse from MSTI called and said she could get us into a doctor in San Francisco, I still felt Seattle was where we needed to be. She got disconnected from Seattle while she'd been waiting on hold.

I got the number from her and made a deal with myself. *I will call and if I don't get through, if I get disconnected, then I will take it as a sign we need to be in California.*

I made the phone call; I was transferred once and got the sweetest voice.

"Swedish Neuroscience Institute."

Shocked I got a real person, I replied, "Hi, this is Jacki Corta, and I am calling about my husband Douglas."

"Yes, I was talking with his nurse in Boise and got disconnected. I am the program director here."

I proceeded to give her all the details of what was happening and how the treatment he received in Boise did not affect the tumor and we needed to see a specialist. "Is there an appointment available to see the neurosurgeon?"

"Yes, you can see him Tuesday. Are you prepared, this appointment could be his pre-op appointment with surgery on Wednesday?"

"Ummm, excuse me? Surgery on Wednesday? They haven't even seen his scans or done any scans!"

She brought me comfort with, "The neurosurgeon you are going to see specializes in glioblastoma tumors and is a phenomenal surgeon. He sees patients like Douglas who have already had surgery to remove the tumor, and due to being a very precise surgeon, he is confident that he can attain getting most, if not all, of the remaining tumor out."

So, our game plan was taking us to Seattle!

We left Monday with an appointment on Tuesday with a neurosurgeon at Swedish Medical Center. We would also see a neuro-oncologist.

Ephesians 6:16

In addition to all this, take up the shield of faith, with which you can extinguish all the flaming arrows of the evil one.

———

We could have questioned and questioned all of these procedures, but it was best for us to hold onto what we were also accomplishing on this journey. I was trusting, believing, and releasing to the Lord, for through Him we were sure to sing the song of victories! This was another step in our journey to get us to the people we needed to get to.

There must be someone in Seattle that also needs Doug and me and our story! I thought as I made all the arrangements for this leg of the journey.

Isaiah 41:10

So do not fear, for I am with you; do not be dismayed, for I am your God. I will strengthen you and help you; I will uphold you with my righteous right hand.

Chapter Twenty-two
Surgery Is Scheduled

CaringBridge Entry
July 22, 2014

It has been a crazy day! We made it to Seattle and met with the most amazing brain tumor advocate! She has researched brain tumors and works with patients on what to expect and gives great information on what to ask the neurosurgeon. She is a support person for patients and their families as well. She is truly a blessing from God bringing us such valid information and peace in being here which was so welcoming with the chaos we have had in the past few days. It is reassuring having her available if we need any support.

We met with the neurosurgeon, and oh my goodness, he is fabulous! He walked into the small patient room we sat in, and we had our introductions.

He asked, "How was your trip over?"

"It was a pleasant drive," came from me.

Doug said, "I am glad to be here."

The neurosurgeon stated, "I looked at your last MRI from Boise and I am very confident in removing this tumor. I am very aggressive with going in and getting it all. We do need you to have some labs done and another MRI. This will be my road map for surgery."

"Will he lose movement of his left side?" I asked as I'd heard this before several times.

Looking at Doug, he answered, "My concern is removing the tumor because I know what it can accomplish. I will know more once I have the MRI and will do my best to have that not affect your mobility but cannot guarantee. There may be some."

With the most determination, Doug said, "You get the tumor out and I can build my strength back up."

He told us it was great to meet us, and he would see us the next day in pre-op.

We then met with the neuro-oncologist, a wise woman! She came in after the neurosurgeon. We had our introductions and she conveyed, "Once you have surgery, we will then make a plan for the treatment you will receive. You are in great hands; he is one of the best neurosurgeons in the country."

They had the pitcher of hope today and poured it into Doug and me to fill us back up. We are both feeling a calmness about being here, as if this is already home, yet we haven't even been here twenty-four hours.

Doug has had labs, and now I am waiting as he is having an MRI. This will be the doctor's "road map" for surgery!

Doug is scheduled for surgery late tomorrow. Our girls are on their way here for it.

Psalms 41:2-3

*The Lord will protect him and preserve his life;
he will bless him in the land and not surrender
him to the desire of his foes. The Lord will sustain
him on his sickbed and restore him from his bed
of illness.*

Next day.

They had Doug scheduled for surgery at 2:00. They felt the surgery
would be about two hours. We checked in at 12:00, and it was nice
to simply step on an elevator and be at check-in. They got him
settled in and the girls went back to give their dad some love. I gave
him a kiss, said "Be strong," and told him that when he wakes up,
he gets to see my cute face!

Two hours passed fast, and I had not heard a word. I checked and
they told me the computer said he was still in surgery. In hearing
that, I had a moment of anxiousness.

As I sat back down in my chair, my phone rang. The OR nurse said
to me, "I wanted you to know we are now getting started with
surgery!"

Two and a half hours behind schedule and I wasn't told before now!
But I could feel the anxiousness leaving my body. They blocked
out for a three-hour surgery, but anticipated it only being two hours,
with an hour in recovery, and then to ICU. We should have news
by 5:00 p.m., which felt like forever!

At about 5:30 the neurosurgeon walked out and said, "The surgery
went well; Doug is doing great so far. The pathology shows there
was tumor regrowth, but I believe I got it all. We will do an MRI to
look at it tonight or in the early morning. I feel it was a success."

Hallelujah Jesus!

I finally got to see Doug around 7:30. He was still very sleepy. He reached for my hand and whispered, "I love you!"

That is what I wanted to hear, his voice speaking to me. He was struggling with nausea but seemed to be good besides that.

The nurse caught me and told me he did have a bit of weakness on the left side of his mouth. The neurosurgeon did not seem concerned, and we would be able to see on his MRI if there had been a stroke or bleeding. His arm strength, leg strength, and sensation were all really good!

We learned from the first brain surgery the primary part of recovery is to maintain low brain activity, so a very quiet environment is essential. The girls came back to see him and as we were all standing around his bed watching him sleep, the nurse came in to check vitals. As she stood there, Doug lifted his left arm in the air. I could see concern on all three of the girls' faces, as they looked at me for some sort of reassurance.

I turned to the nurse, "Is his IV bothering him?"

She gently spoke, "Douglas, does your arm feel funny or feel like it is doing weird things?"

With very little hesitation, he said, "No, I'm checking to make sure it works!"

The girls and I giggled! Poor guy was so scared he was going to lose movement on his left side!

―――――――――

We have not had the MRI, yet. Doug's nausea has taken some time to get over. He has been resting quite well. He opened his eyes briefly, and I told him to remember what Stewart Scott said in his speech, "When I need to rest, I rest, and all my family and supporters do all the fighting for me!" So, rest my love, rest and heal!

Psalms 30:2

*O Lord my God, I called to you for help and you
healed me.*

Doug's nausea took quite a while to subside, but finally did. His
mom, dad, and my mom sat with him most of the time on our third
day while Shanan and I took the girls to Pike's Market and dinner.
They were needing to get out of the hospital and have some much-
needed mom time. There has not been enough one-on-one time with
the girls. It was good for all of us!

I knew Doug was doing okay when I asked him if there was
anything he wanted, and he softly said, "World peace."

His MRI showed no sign of stroke or bleeding, and they got all the
tumor regrowth! *Thank you, Jesus, we are giving glory to God!* We
are praying no microscopic tumor starts growing!

The tumor Doug has is very aggressive and the smallest of pieces
could grow! I am still believing by the grace of God this will not
happen! I am a stronger person emotionally and in my faith because
of what I am experiencing. We are never sure what path our journey
might take, but we can be in control of how we react to the journey
and how we learn from it. Even when we don't really want to, we
need to embrace it and allow God to guide us! He will never fail us!

Chapter Twenty-three

Long Week

Doug was extremely sick and weak once we arrived home from Seattle. After getting on a new supplement program and some reflexology sessions through our wellness clinic, he seemed to be doing better. But he was not being a very good patient that time around. He was a bit impatient! He wanted to be walking farther than he was, he would have liked to have more strength than he had, and he wished he wasn't experiencing so much brain fog.

I had to tell him numerous times he was just a week out of surgery, that it was *brain* surgery, and he needed to settle down and rest.

In our times of trials, we have turned to God, which is exactly what we *should* do, but where we get frustrated is when we ask for God to help us, guide us, and show us and we feel it is not happening fast enough. We were looking for big signs from Him.

What we needed to learn first was we should not wait for a trial to turn to God. We needed to turn to Him every day. So I stopped looking for big signs from Him. The Lord is always right next to us, giving us guidance and support.

I felt we were exactly where we were supposed to be, but still needed confirmation. Speaking to the neurosurgeon about the surgery and Doug's apprehension about losing movement of his left side, I had asked that if he needed to make a decision about taking more of the tumor, would he pause surgery and come talk to me before he needed to do it?

He reached down and touched my knee and said, "I already have a game plan!"

That was the Lord speaking through the doctor! My God knew that was my lingo, and it was His way of saying, "Jacki, I am here with you, you are in the place I have guided you to be, now you need to relax and trust."

I understood that we didn't always have to look for the big signs from God, we could rely on our feelings of Him next to us. It is the butterfly that won't leave you alone, it is the glimpse of the sunset or the sunrise, it might be the open parking spot in a full lot. We must trust ourselves, so when we might "think" we feel Him, KNOW IT!

Joshua 1:9

Have I not commanded you? Be strong and courageous. Do not be terrified; do not be discouraged, for the Lord your God will be with you wherever you go.

Once we got back from Seattle, life picked up speed! Doug started another treatment, the girls registered for school, I was working at both businesses, I took a trip to the mountains to pick huckleberries, Bent took her senior pictures, we had a golf scramble fundraiser, we took Z back to Weber State, Bentli and Demi started school, and I just tried to remember to breathe!

The treatment was a bit of an adjustment. Along with trying to heal from surgery, the meds made Doug tired. He had not been cleared to drive, which really frustrated him, but he was slowly getting stronger each day.

This second surgery and recovery was quite different and seemed to have taken a bit more out of him. But he was fighting hard to gain all his strength back so he could get back to doing the things he loves.

We held a golf scramble fundraiser for Doug and our family. Oh my gosh, it was a beautiful day and such an amazing turnout. Doug and I dallied along the golf course in a golf cart. We did our best to meet each team that was playing! It was very humbling to see all the support for my husband. We were feeling very blessed!

The next day, Doug and I drove down with Z to Weber State to get her moved in. What a great time we had with her. It was an exhausting weekend for Doug. But what a trooper, he hung with us all weekend. Z seemed to have grown so much over the summer; what an amazing young lady she had turned into.

As we returned home Sunday evening, Doug and I ended up on the deck bawling our eyes out! I had thought this year was going to be easier, but boy was I mistaken. We spent all these years raising our children to spread their wings and fly on their own. Then when they reached that moment of flight, I wanted to call them back to the nest!

Not really. It brought me joy to watch Z fly on her own. I just wanted her—and the others—to remember how to fly home occasionally.

What a crazy year I had ahead of me. Bentli was a senior at Eagle High and Demi, my baby, was a freshman! Oh, the emotions of having a senior had already started. I bawled all the way through previewing her senior pictures. As I thought about Z at college, I cried in anticipation, knowing Bentli will be gone next year, as well.

Mark 11:24

Therefore I tell you, whatever you ask for in prayer, believe that you have received it, and it will be yours.

Chapter Twenty-four

Roller Coaster...

We spent Labor Day weekend over in Halfway, Oregon with my sister and her family. What a fun time relaxing, going to the rodeo, and watching the fawns frolic in their backyard.

Then, on the following Monday, Doug and I took off for Seattle.

Doug had an MRI and his labs drawn, and then we saw his neuro-oncologist. As she walked in, I experienced the tremendous butterflies that sometimes overtook me with the anticipation of what she would say to us. As I sat there, in my head I kept repeating, *Good news, no growth, good news, no growth...*

Then she spoke: "It looks like the tumor has possibly started to grow."

I looked over at Doug and saw heartache billowing up to his face. I took a deep breath to call my inner warrior to the helm.

The doctor continued, "The chemo he is on doesn't usually work on these tumors. We will need to change his chemo treatment."

I felt like I'd been punched in the gut.

The doctor ordered a CT scan before we left Seattle to check for any bleeding because the new chemo had the potential side effect of hemorrhaging. If Doug had any bleeding, we would have to go another route.

The CT scan was quick, and we were back on the road for Idaho. We both felt exhausted. It's strange—all there is to do is sit in a waiting area, sit in a doctor's office, sit and listen, but we felt like we ran a marathon.

Doug and I discussed how we *needed* a bit of good news, a little glimpse of hope. I told him right then, "My prayer for the next two months is for hope and guidance. For there to be a bit of glory to us." I promised him I would pray this prayer until the next MRI.

Soon after we got home, we received the CT results. Doug did have some post-surgery bleeding, meaning we were going to have to change chemo courses, again. The good news? That spot might not be tumor growth, it could be blood.

Oh my gosh! Amen Jesus! That is what I needed to hear. A bit of hope, a bit of good news was what we'd *just* asked for and what we so desperately needed. At this point, we grabbed and took whatever we could!

When I told Doug, his whole demeanor changed. It was time to change our prayer, and to be as specific as possible: We would pray that in four weeks, the tumor is stable and still not growing.

We celebrated that night. It was what we needed at that moment because our emotions had been somewhat of a roller coaster that past week!

We were set to return to Seattle in October. We were believing in a good MRI, with no change in his tumor. I knew the Lord was by our side, guiding us through this part of our journey, which we knew would have some challenges. We were strong in our faith.

I was asked daily how I was doing, or people told me that I was so strong. But I did have moments of weakness, days where I barely put one foot in front of the other to get from wake up to bedtime.

I honestly thought I was doing pretty darn good for the most part. I was cherishing each day as they came. If I was completely honest,

I would have admitted being tired of doctors' appointments, phone calls, decisions, results, and the unknown. But all of that was outweighed by the quiet evenings snuggling on the couch with my husband, the soft *I love you*s, every minute I got to be blessed with Doug by my side, and the strong presence of the Lord in my life.

My faith, along with the special people who answered the phone at all hours of the day, got me through some of the hardest days. It was my army of people praying for our family that made my legs strong when they became weak. It took the whole Team Corta to fight that fight! I believed, I trusted, I allowed the Lord to work miracles on my husband. I gave all the glory to God in every big and small victory we achieved!

Acts 3:16

By faith in the name of Jesus, this man whom you see and know was made strong. It is Jesus's name and the faith that comes through him that has given this complete healing to him, as you can all see.

Chapter Twenty-five

We All Have a Story

CaringBridge Entry
September 12, 2014

Interesting as it may be, I have witnessed some powerful things these past few days and weeks about other people's stories. I think there are times when I get so wrapped up in my own story, I am unaware of what is happening around me. Well, these last few days and weeks, I have tried to be more aware of others' stories, and I am amazed at what I have learned, or what the Lord keeps showing me.

I have a beautiful friend who will send me a text message every so often to say, "I was thinking about you today."

Simple, but to me, it is very powerful. She has been through a bit of what I am going through; the story is different, but we've both traveled the battle of cancer, only she was fighting with her dad. She has her own story of trials and joys, moments of weakness and times of being the rock for everyone else.

It is when she looks me in the face—I can almost feel her pain— and she gives me a hug and says, "Call me anytime. We can go to lunch, we can visit, or we can sit and cry." It is in those moments that I feel her story and mine might be a bit the same.

Her dad was welcomed home by Jesus, leaving behind her beautiful mom, and my beautiful friend is missing her dad. I only know bits of her story, but I am awakened when she says she is thinking about me; it is from her soul that she truly cares, and someone who knows of what I am going through.

As I was scrolling through Facebook today, I noticed a post. It was by a girl I went to high school with. It truly blew me away.

I watched this video of a young man learning to bend over and pick up a very large beach ball. It was a struggle for him to grab the ball, but he kept his determination and reached the ball and lifted it up as he sat back down. His therapist was by his side the whole time.

I heard of this boy's story from the news and the newspaper. This young man was playing football last year when he was paralyzed. He has fought very hard to regain mobility; what an example of fighting. This warmed my heart and reinforced my faith.

———————

Stories like that remind me of others. Last winter I attended a basketball game that honored a teacher and coach. I had never seen Eagle High packed that way. Every seat was filled. It was all for this sweet young family whose dad was diagnosed with esophageal cancer.

As they announced the family and the dad spoke to the crowd, I was overcome by emotions for this poor wife with two young babies.

I remember thinking, *I will say a prayer for this family*, and then I went to church and added them to our prayer team. *Our stories are different yet so close in nature. I feel your pain, I cry your tears, I pray for you and your husband.*

I share these stories because I feel they have been placed in my path for numerous reasons. We go through our daily routines thinking about our own story or that we are the only ones.

Don't get me wrong, it is fine to get caught up in our stories, but we need to realize everyone has a story. It might not be as big or as bad or as good, but we all have a story to tell. They all have special meanings. I encourage everyone to share their story. It's why you are holding this book.

All stories are important, and they should be shared. Our stories all have the capability of reaching one soul and though we may never even know we have reached them, it matters.

Ephesians 4:29

Do not let any unwholesome talk come out of your mouths, but only what is helpful for building others up according to their needs, that it may benefit those who listen.

Chapter Twenty-six

It Has Been Chaotic!

CaringBridge Entry
Late September

Just when I think life is going to settle a bit, it goes full-on busy again! Busy with fun, appointments, kids, and jobs! I would not trade it for anything—well maybe a few days of quiet time. I might like that for a moment!

Doug is handling the new chemo quite well. His counts have been fairly good until this last week. They have now dropped low enough that he will not start back on the chemo until his counts come up. We are hoping by next weekend!

He has been going down to our restaurant, Doug's Burger Den, on Friday mornings to have coffee and breakfast and BS with the customers who have missed him. I realized a lot of the customers that frequent the restaurant came in more for the conversation with Doug than for the food. It has shown me what a family all the customers have become. We thought we opened a restaurant for people to enjoy the food—which they do—but more importantly, they come for the relationships that have formed over the years. Seeing them enjoy the time with Doug brightens my day.

When regulars ask, "How is he doing?" I can see the compassion they have for my husband. When Doug started coming down on Fridays, the hugs, the smiles, and the *it is so good to see you*s touched my heart. So many people care for him without us even knowing it. It has been good for Doug to come down, and it has been good for customers to see him!

Life seems to show us new things every day. Things we want to see and experience, and things we might think we don't need to see, or know about, but in all reality, they also benefit us. In the last seven months, my life has been turned upside down. But all the while, I have learned so much. I am capable of more than I ever thought I could achieve.

My faith is something I have always had, but when I truly rely on it, it only strengthens, and God shows himself. Vulnerability can be a scary thing, but when we allow ourselves to be vulnerable, we are open to new experiences.

Family and friends become present in our journey. They give support, they provide a safe place, and they have their own dealings with the journey we are on, causing some desolation. I have learned that in the turmoil of a diagnosis and the wake of treatment, three young girls can display grit, tenacity, courage, and be scared to death all at the same time.

As Doug hit a very angry moment a few weeks ago, I allowed and encouraged him to feel it. I stood there and watched as he slammed a chair and threw it off our deck, screaming in anger.

I walked up to him, strengthening my own armor; he put his head on my shoulder and cried. I said to him, "This is so healthy for you. This is normal for you to feel all these emotions. I am so proud of you for not holding this in!"

We discussed all the positive things that have come from being diagnosed with brain cancer.

Positive things? Let me explain. Before, I attended church, but I was not dutiful; I believed in the Lord, but I did not share my beliefs with anyone.

Before, Doug was harder; now he sees the importance of life. The diagnosis has softened him.

Before, we took each other for granted; now we are grateful for each other. Before, *things* were important, now *time* is important; before, we thought we were close and loved each other, now we KNOW how close we are and how much we truly love each other.

I am standing firm in my faith that the Lord has a plan, one we cannot see yet. I am believing in miracles, I am believing by the grace of God, healing hands will be laid upon Doug. I am trusting that this season will pass and a new one will blossom.

We head back to Seattle soon for an MRI to compare to his last one. We are believing the tumor is stable.

Chapter Twenty-seven

Just Back from Seattle

Monday morning, Doug, Shanan, and I took off for Seattle. We seemed to make good time, knowing we had to get past the rock blasting at Snoqualmie Pass. It started at 8:00 p.m. on all our other trips.

As we approached the first road sign it stated, "Temporary road closure due to rock blasting starting at 6:00 p.m.!" *WHAT... 6:00!* I looked down at the clock to see 6:08 p.m., and we began to speed a bit. I was hoping the machines hadn't started on time—wishful thinking on my part.

We spent forty-five minutes at a standstill, in the most beautiful, peaceful location in the mountains. The air was brisk, the smell of the pines filled the car.

I felt Doug's energy start to shift—not so upbeat, a bit quieter. This seemed to happen each time we went to Seattle, the closer we got the quieter he became.

As we walked into the hospital, I fully felt Doug's anxiety. I guess I understood where he was coming from, but I was trying to shift the energy in hopes it would feel more peaceful, more positive; I thought being a little calmer would help with his anxiety.

We got to the room and settled into bed. I watched the clock until about 2:30 a.m. I guess it was good timing because Doug and Shanan said they watched it from 4:00 until 6:30 a.m.! As we got ready, I suggested we read our daily devotional.

As I read it out loud to Doug, I saw a shift in him. We both felt a calmness come over us.

Doug checked in at 7:30 with his MRI at 8:00. I felt his anxiety build as we rode the elevator to the basement. The nurse came out and got him, and he leaned over and gave me a kiss.

I said, "I will see you in a bit." I rode the elevator up alone, saying a prayer in my head.

I found myself this time trying to not get discouraged. I had been doing my best to stay positive but had found that with every trip to Seattle, we had gotten a bit of discouraging news. So, this time, I talked to God and said I would be prepared for whatever news we got.

This was my journey, and I would go with whatever He was putting in front of me. I was joyful for the health Doug had at that time and for the strength he was showing. If we got bad news, I would not allow it to bring me down. I would stand firm in my faith and look forward to whatever we needed to do. I felt assured that this time I would stay strong.

It was always the waiting that got to me, so I began to pray again.

Doug returned to the patient room and the nurse started off with question after question about his vitals. It was getting so routine that I was sick of it all. As the nurse finished up, I felt my anxiety and overall uneasy feelings increasing.

She walked out and we sat, waiting for the doctor to come in. What was only about fifteen minutes felt like five hours; my mind ran like a herd of horses. I mentally chanted, *MRI is good! MRI is good! MRI is good!* I said quick little prayers, asking for good news; we sure needed it.

Doug's whole demeanor was going south the longer we waited. As the time went on, I finally had myself convinced the report was not good and it was taking her that long to get the nerve to come in and tell us.

It's amazing what we allow our minds to do to us. My stomach was in knots, the fluttering in my chest would not go away. The silence in the room was almost eerie, but I felt that was what Doug wanted, so we sat in silence.

When the doctor walked in, the lump in my throat huge, my heart began to race, and the anticipation consumed me. In what was about sixty seconds, I tried to figure out her body language regarding what she was about to say.

She smiled when she walked in: *Is that good, or is she trying to comfort us?* She didn't cross her legs when she sat down: *Is she more tense because it is not good?*

She looked at Doug and asked how he felt: *Is that because she knows the MRI is not good?*

She asked how I was: *Is that because she is about to tell me something I don't want to hear?*

And then she spoke, "The MRI shows mixed things." My heart was racing faster. "The spot we saw in the last MRI looks stable and even a bit smaller." *Amen!* "But there is a new spot that has shown up; it is very small, and I want to do radiation so we can get it."

Deep breath, deep breath, breathe, Jack, breathe.

She told us we had an appointment with a radiation oncologist at 1:00 p.m. to get it all lined out. She wanted his radiation done within two weeks, with another MRI in eight weeks.

As we left her office, we felt very positive. We walked to have lunch before we had to be at the next appointment.

When it was time, a sweet nurse came out and got us and took us into a room with a round table for us all to sit at with the computer screen up, so we could see his MRI pictures. The radiation oncologist walked in, shook all our hands, sat down in the chair, leaned way back in it, crossed his arms, and asked us what questions we had for him.

Wait what? He didn't come in here and fill us with a ton of information, some of which we probably wouldn't understand, using words we've never heard of. Instead, he was down to earth, spoke our language, and wanted to know our concerns before he even said a word. I already liked this guy!

He answered all of our questions and gave us all the information we needed. He wanted to know about Doug—Doug the man, not Doug and his tumor. He asked him what he did, how long he had been doing it, how old his girls were, what they did, where they were. He loved that Doug owned a restaurant, he wanted to know where it was, what it was called, and what he served. I was amazed! He truly wanted to know Doug! He made Doug feel seen as a man and that brought some peace to me.

We were in his office for two hours; they worked Doug in so he could get his radiation mask made and a CT scan done. When Doug came out from having the mask made, there was panic on his face.

I asked, "Are you okay?"

He said, "Forty minutes, Jack, I don't know if I can do it. He isn't cutting out the eyes for me to see."

I said, "For forty minutes you lay there with your eyes closed so you can't see the mask over them." I reassured him trying to make it as light as possible, "One time, dear, you only have to do it one time!"

I am not sure I was convincing enough. The doubt he experienced radiated through his hand as I held it. We talked about the MRI showing the one spot stable or even smaller and what a victory that was. Maybe a small victory, but a victory we had not had in a while.

Doug squeezed my hand as he leaned in and kissed my cheek. Then he whispered, "Thanks for being so strong, Jack."

1 Thessalonians 5:18

Give thanks in all circumstances, for this is God's will for you in Christ Jesus.

———————

CaringBridge Entry
October 21, 2014

We are standing firm, believing and trusting that this grand journey we are on will have more victories to be announced!

My prayer today is for safe travels, calm nerves, open doors. My prayer is also for us to feel the presence of the Lord with us, for the radiation to destroy the tumor, that Doug keeps pushing forward with this amazing attitude, that my knees don't go weak, and that my faith be stronger.

Doug and I spent the day in downtown Seattle, it was a beautiful day. We walked, we sat, we laughed, we walked more, we had lunch, we walked, we walked, oh, and we walked. We made it to his appointment early. As they came out to get him, I asked if I could go back and take some pictures of the machine/room.

They were very accommodating and allowed me to go back and take a few photos. What a massive machine! The actual radiation lasted about forty minutes, then we met with the doctor who showed us the most precise pictures of where the very high dose of radiation was applied. I was amazed by the technology and science behind it all.

Once we made it home, Z called.

I answered, cinching up my armor to appear much stronger than I felt, "Hey sis, how are you?"

"Good, how was Seattle?" She replied but I could tell she wanted and wished this wasn't a loaded question.

WHEN YOUR **MIRACLE** *Doesn't Come*

"It was fine. How were your games?" Oh, how we wished we had the freedom to travel to her games instead of the back and forth to Seattle.

"They were good." She then shared how she played, how the team played, and certain plays that stood out, as well as the hits she had. "Mom, I have to tell you what happened after the game."

"Oh gosh, is everything okay, sis?" It felt like it was, but because of all our stuff, I tentatively awaited her reply.

"Yes, Mom! After the game we met as a team in the outfield so the coaches could talk about the games, how they went and stuff, like always. Then Coach A said, 'We have a tribute we need to do.' Mom, Coach said to us all, 'We are a team. A team fights together. We are a family, and family sticks together. And when we need to, we fight for each other.' And then my dearest teammate joined Coach and they pulled out bracelets for everyone that said Team Corta on them!"

Extreme gratitude filled every ounce of me, knowing this coach and program cared so deeply for the battle my girl was going through.

When Doug started his fight, there were bracelets made that read TEAM CORTA on one side and OVERCOMING ADVERSITY on the other side. They were given to teams that Doug's high school team played against and were also sold to show support.

Z continued, "Mom, I bawled, like the whole ugly cry. I was so shocked; I could not stop crying. The whole team was crying. They are all wearing Dad's bracelets! Can you believe they would do that for me?"

I, through teary eyes replied with, "Z, that is what TEAM is all about!"

I was so honored and blessed that her team supported and backed my girl when I held up everything at home. She had such a great team with an amazing leader, which created the community and family she needed while her dad fought cancer. It brought this momma a whole bunch of peace.

When Z told the story to her dad, his voice cracked, and tears began to well in his eyes.

———————

Later that week.

Church on Sunday was super powerful for me. I turned all the things over to Him and released what I had been grasping onto. Funny how we think we need to keep a hold, when releasing whatever it may be is what frees us.

My life got a bit busy, but I realized I must make a conscious decision, daily, to say my prayers, read my devotional, sit in silence, and talk to the Lord. Doug's diagnosis turned my life upside down, but in the process of being upside down, the Lord reached down, grabbed my hand, and turned me upright. He told me to stand tall, stand firm in my faith, and stand next to Him and to stay upright through all that is thrown at me.

Psalms 107:20

He sent forth his word and healed them; he rescued them from the grave.

Chapter Twenty-eight

Today, I Wept

CaringBridge Entry
November 18, 2014

Today has been a bit harder for me. I have a dear friend that I spoke to one day when it was not a good day. She said to me, "Jacki you need to listen to God. Sit in silence and hear what He says."

I responded, "He said, 'Weep my child, weep!'"

So, today, I am weeping! My heart is sad today. I know I am a warrior; I know I am strong; I know I have the faith, but I also know I have these sensitive emotions that have come to the surface!

My dad is in the early stages of Alzheimer's and has not been doing very well. And my husband—my best friend and soulmate—is battling the biggest battle he will ever face. Today, I am feeling like I am losing the two most important men in my life; so today, I weep.

It amazes me how something can consume a person every day. Every day I deal with cancer, it is never far from my thoughts. Bills are still coming in, meds are taken daily, appointments are being scheduled, doctors are calling, labs are being done, and I am constantly watching Doug's every move. *Has he changed? Are things okay? Is he not feeling well? Why is he not feeling well?*

Does he need something from me? Can I help in any way? Every day cancer is in my thoughts.

I am realizing how much our lives have changed since the diagnosis. I see people enjoying things, doing things, or going places, and I catch myself wondering what their story is. Then, I catch myself a bit sad that my journey right now does not include enjoying those things, doing those things, or going to those places.

Am I being selfish? Maybe. But I allow myself to be, if only for a moment. Life is different when in the path of cancer. I never truly realized how it would change my life. I do look at things, people, and situations a lot differently now.

I believe I am going with a new outlook, maybe not that cancer has consumed me, but it has joined our family.

Dear Brain Cancer,

WELCOME TO THE FAMILY! You have joined five of the most amazing people you could have picked. I am sorry I did not welcome you with open arms, and it has taken me nine months to actually get around to greeting you.

We five have an extremely tight bond and letting you in was a bit hard. We were already complete, so you see our resistance. We are a family of faith, so you need to know we pray for each other and for everyone's well-being.

One of the biggest prayers we say is for you to actually leave our family. Your visit has been long enough, and we can do without you being around.

I always tell my girls, you are exactly where you are supposed to be at the exact time, so you, Cancer, are here for a reason.

Now, we might not fully know your reason for being here, and we understand there might be more lessons to be learned from you. My eyes are open to all lessons. Doug's eyes are open to all lessons, and those three beauties I call my girls, their eyes are also wide open to all lessons.

See, you didn't even know it, but we have already learned so much from you. There is a part of me that needs to thank you. Thank you for rejuvenating my faith. Thank you for reminding us five that life is really good, being a family, home on the couch. Thank you for showing us life is not about materialistic things, it's about living a Christ-filled life with each other.

While I never wanted to meet you, and I don't want you to stay, I needed to let you know how I feel about you.

In Christ,

Jacki

So, as I had my weeping party that day, I also came to terms with how it was okay to have a day to weep. I don't have to always be so strong. When we trust and engage in Christ, He can do all things. That day, it was what carried me!

As Thanksgiving loomed, I was reminded to stop for a moment each day and be thankful for something, someone, or some situation. I said a quick prayer for them, and I looked deeply at what I might be thankful for. I was thankful that year for the tender kisses from Doug that I got daily, and the snuggling on the couch every night before bed. I was thankful that I saw the sun shining a bit brighter on certain days. I looked up at the trees and the hills and saw complete beauty. God was shining all around us! I was thankful for the journey I was on. It put life and life's importance clearly in my path.

Philippians 4:4-7

Rejoice in the Lord always. I will say it again:
Rejoice! Let your gentleness be evident to all.
The Lord is near. Do not be anxious about
anything, but in everything, by prayer and
petition, with thanksgiving, present your requests
to God. And the peace of God, which transcends
all understanding, will guard your hearts and
your minds in Christ Jesus.

Chapter Twenty-nine

Just Returned from Seattle

CaringBridge Entry
December 5, 2014

Doug had his MRI this morning in Seattle. As always, we walked in with high hopes they would tell us that the MRI shows the tumor is stable.

This hasn't happened before, and unfortunately, it didn't happen this time either! I seem to get myself all worked up waiting for the oncologist to walk in to give us the results.

She entered the room. "Hey you guys, how are you doing?"

Doug stayed silent as I said, "We are good."

She quickly stated, "The MRI shows two new spots of growth."

Ughh, that is not what we wanted to hear. We are feeling deflated, socked in the jaw, punched in the gut.

The chemo Doug is taking is obviously not working, so it is time to try another cocktail of chemo. They are going to do a six- to eight-hour procedure where they put a frame around Doug's head, which is screwed into his skull to hold it in place. They do a CT scan to locate the exact spots, and then write up their plan of attack. Doug then goes in for treatment that takes about one hour. They will then remove the screws and frame and he will be in recovery for a bit.

Was this the news we were hoping for? NO, but I am feeling this is one more step God needs us to take to get us to where we need to be.

I could sit here and ask why. Why more, why us, why again, why, why, *why*, but asking gives us no answers, nor does it solve anything. *Why is this happening?* Because God has a plan for our lives bigger than what we can see.

I am believing His plan has complete healing for Doug, but there is more to our journey we need to go through. Is it hard? Yes! Is it sometimes not fun? Yes! Does it sometimes feel challenging? Yes! Is it easier when I lean on God? Yes! Is it more comforting with the Lord near me? Yes! This is why I say, "Spirit, lead me where my trust is without borders! Without borders I am allowing Him to do all things through me, for me, with me. I am trusting in Him with all things! And I am going wherever He calls me."

He might call us where we think we don't need to go. But my God knows exactly where I need to be, and wherever He calls me is where I need to be and will be. Because wherever He calls me, He will be right next to me.

It's important that we stop questioning where we are in our journey and allow God to speak to our hearts. We must learn from the experiences and give glory to God at the end results.

We must understand that sometimes the result is not what we want to be the ending. But God has another chapter to write. While we are going through those chapters of our lives, we can't sit back at the chapter where we want things to end, we have to push forward to the final chapter that God has in store. Although it may be extremely hard to attain this, and we may want to dig our heels in at the chapter where we are, trust me. I have been there digging them in, not wanting to see what He had in store.

I don't mean the final chapter of life, I mean the final chapter in whatever might be happening right now, what a person may be struggling with right now, or even questioning right now. See, if I was in charge of the writing, my end would have been nine months ago: Doug has a tumor, we had surgery and it was removed, and all is good. But that's my story, not the Lord's—He has more chapters for me to write.

God is good! Let me say why I feel God is so good. With all I have gone through these last nine months, Christ has been put front and center in my life. My lenses have been wiped clean, and I see the good in all things cleansed.

My husband is still strong, still loving, still funny, still the BEST DAD my three girls could ever ask for. My husband has become the man of faith that I always knew him to be. But now, he shares his faith boldly. God is good because I am still learning, and He is still teaching!

Jeremiah 17:7

But blessed is the man who trusts in the Lord, whose confidence is in him.

———————

Last week, Doug was struggling. Z called to talk to him, and they visited for quite a while. The next morning, Doug woke up to this text that came in at 1:30 a.m. from Z.

Hopefully you're asleep and this doesn't wake you up. I was thinking about you tonight as I was doing my homework and I figured I'd share my thoughts. You were frustrated and scared today, now yesterday, which is totally acceptable, but that was yesterday. Today is a new day! Yesterday's home runs don't win today's games, right? Well yesterday's strikeouts don't win today's game either! You always told me not to get discouraged, keep working your ass off and it will pay off, someone will notice you. Well, same goes for you except you're going to work your ass off at enjoying life and being happy. Make everyday a good day, no exceptions. Granted, good days will turn into bad days, but don't make it a bad couple of days. I want you to find the good in each day! :) I love you Dad :) you deserve to be happy more than anyone. Sometimes, we are the only one that can make that happen! It's a choice :)

When Doug read me this, I bawled my eyes out! As parents, we preach and preach and hope they are listening! Hoping they will grow to be true, be an influence, and get what life is about. This shows me she was listening! At that moment of the text, Z was much wiser than Doug and me. And I am grateful for that.

Exodus 20:12

Honor your father and your mother, so that you may live long in the land the Lord your God is giving you.

Chapter Thirty

Oh My...

We were headed to Seattle for Doug's radiation treatment. This trip had us leaving on Thursday night, treatment on Friday, with our flight home Friday night. It was so nice we had Z with us.

On the way to check-in, Z said, "Dad, this is going to be so fun!"

His response, "Oh yeah, Z, having something screwed to my head is way too much fun!"

Our flight was delayed thirty minutes. Once we got on board, the pilot said to us, "Hope you all used the restroom before boarding because the smoothest part of the flight will be right here. We will not be roaming the cabin tonight into Seattle!"

I wanted to get off the plane. I am not a very good flier, and his announcement did not sit well with me. But off we went! It was a little bumpy out of Boise, then some unexpected smooth air. That is what you would call the calm before the storm!

The last thirty minutes into Seattle, I knew we were either rolling or nose diving. My palms began to sweat, I said a few prayers. We bobbled back and forth and finally hit the ground. We literally hit the ground so hard that Z hit her head on the seat in front of her. Once we had slowed down, the cabin erupted in cheering and clapping. Doug ended up very sick with motion sickness. People were throwing up in the airport once we got off. I was so glad to be on the ground.

We got up at 5:30 a.m. to get to the hospital check-in at 6:30 a.m. Doug was given anxiety meds to keep him calm.

The doctor walked in to go over the procedure.

"Good morning." He looked at me and said, "Is this your sister?"

With giggles from us all I said, "No this is our oldest daughter Z, but thank you for the compliment."

He continued, "There are actually three very small spots. One is deeper in the back of the cavity and the other two are in the lining of the brain. It is very unusual, but not to worry, maybe Doug was meant to be unusual."

I spoke up and said, "We Cortas don't like to do the norm."

They asked Z and me to leave while they put the frame on Doug. I was not prepared for what it was going look like. Even though I knew what it consisted of, seeing four screws placed into Doug's forehead and the back of his head with a thick metal halo attached caused me to feel uneasy. It might have been fear of the unknown again or the sheer fact I hated seeing the love of my life going through this.

Off to the CT he went. Once he got back, they mounted a bubble-like thing on top of the frame. We joked he looked like George Jetson! I was quite amazed.

They took measurements of all different angles. The nurse kept saying the measurements while another nurse wrote them down.

As she was calling them out, Doug said, "It sounds like you are playing Battleship up there."

The treatment was an hour and forty-five minutes. After treatment, they came in and removed the frame and stuck four Band-aids on the spots where the screws had been.

The best part of the seven-and-a-half-hour appointment was the nurse and doctor both said it was so nice my sister came with us.

After we got home, I felt a bit more exhausted, a bit more at my wits end, struggling a bit more. That night, I was pushed to where I felt like I was hanging at the very end of the rope. Still holding on but feeling like it was the tiniest of strings. I recognized I had been carrying a lot of stress and holding onto the pressure of keeping it all together for everyone. I was overwhelmed with my plate becoming very full.

Demi was playing basketball at the high school. I am so passionate about the game, and I was so proud of how well she was playing. It was like she finally came into her game, realizing what she could accomplish.

Well one night, about two minutes into the game, she stood in front of a player and took a charge! I jumped up cheering, because I see taking a charge as being so selfless. As she got to the other end of the court, she began to cry.

Okay wait, Demi has the highest pain tolerance I have ever seen. A sub was sent in, and she sat on the bench crying. The trainer went over, by then Demi thought she was good to keep playing. She went back into the game; a pass was sent her way and she couldn't catch it. The pain prompted the tears again. Off the court she went, ice wrapped around her wrist.

After the game, Doug and my mom took her to have an X-ray. She returned to the gym in a cast, *Oh MY!* She broke a bone in her right arm behind her wrist and had to see an orthopedic surgeon.

As I walked up to my sweet baby, her eyes welling with tears, I hugged her. She sunk into my chest sobbing. I held her for a moment and then I softly said to her, "Sister, we have lessons to be learned. I know it sucks, but there are lessons to be learned." I kissed the top of her head and told her I loved her guts and was so dang proud of her.

I am going to be very honest. I walked into the empty locker room and wanted to sit and cry my eyes out. For that moment, I felt weak, really weak. You know that quote, "God will only give you what you can handle"? I begged to differ that night because I'm not sure what He saw in me, but I was not sure how much more I could handle. I was feeling very, very defeated.

Good, I needed a bit of good to be put in my family. It seemed like every corner we turned, we saw the good in the distance and then a mountain of adversity slammed us in our faces. I was not sure how much more I could endure.

Tonight, I am allowing myself to be weak, sad, hopeless, and not have one ounce of fight in me. Tonight, I am throwing up my arms and surrendering.

1 Peter 5:7

Cast all your anxiety on him because he cares for you.

I had no idea a person could have enough tears to cry for fifteen hours! But I can testify that I had had enough! When I threw up my arms and surrendered, I bawled for fifteen hours. The poor girls wanted to know what was going on. I said, "I can't stop crying. It is going to be a bad day."

I was at a loss when they said Demi broke her arm. I was pushed to the very edge of the cliff, not sure how I was not going to fall off.

Honestly, at first, I wanted to be pissed, scream "this is not fair!" but this little voice spoke up and reminded me of what I say to my girls. "Life is not fair. But we have a choice how we handle the unfairness thrown at us. Do we sit and bask in it, or do we rise above it, grasping onto the lesson in it? What do we do with the unfairness? That's the challenge."

Crap, why did I use that line on my girls? I had to listen to my own words of wisdom and apply them to my life. I had to remind myself of what I told Demi while she sobbed in my chest: *lessons to be learned, there are lessons to be learned.*

Isaiah 30:20-21

Although the Lord gives you the bread of adversity and the water of affliction, your teachers will be hidden no more; with your own eyes you will see them. Whether you turn to the right or to the left, your ears will hear a voice behind you, saying, "This is the way; walk in it."

I always believed things happen for a reason. We are tested, we are challenged, we have a lesson to learn, but never have I thought a problem would be a rich opportunity.

I had one of the toughest weeks that week, but also was blessed beyond measure. I was very weak and very vulnerable throughout most of it, and it was okay. But I soon decided I had to not sit on the edge of that cliff anymore, I needed to step back and keep fighting.

I think we get so wrapped up in always being so strong, so tough, so faithful, that we forget we can actually fall and throw a fit, if needed. But then it's important to make the choice to sit on the edge of that cliff or step back and stand up and fight the good fight. I knew I would have more weak days ahead, more not-so-great moments, but I also knew I would have big victories to write about in my near future.

Chapter Thirty-one

Happy New Year!

Christmas was such a great time. I loved having family around, with all the laughing, loving, and time together. That year was extra special.

As I sat there on New Year's Eve pondering over the year, here are some things I came up with.

Let me say, I could sit here and say, "Goodbye, I am glad to see you go," but I actually am not saying that at all. There were so many things the year brought to us.

My oldest daughter lived out a dream she had had since she was ten; she played in her first collegiate softball game.

I was asked to join the coaching staff at Eagle High for the girls' basketball program (a dream I have had since forever!).

Bentli started her senior year (*where did my little girl go?*).

Demi started high school (*now, truly, where did my baby go?*)!

I was blessed with the most amazing clients I get to see every week. I was challenged by a new business (Doug's Burger Den). And Doug was able to finally stop working seven days a week. Now, I am not sure if he would have said that was good, but I believe it was.

That year brought cancer front and center in our lives. But in the process, it also returned my faith in Christ. It showed me how strong I could be and also how weak I could be. It gave me the courage to step out of my comfort zone and share with thousands of people my journey. It gave me the most amazing support group of people a girl could ask for; it allowed me to see the true people and the not-so-true people in my life.

When intense situations happen, we have no control over how others will handle them or how people will treat us. It can cause others to shine in a way that is not beneficial to our journey. In our case, I believe it was how they dealt with the struggle they were going through with Doug's diagnosis of brain cancer. It taught me to place boundaries to protect myself.

Most would say that with all I had been dealt in that year, it must be chalked up to being the worst or one of the worst years of my life.

I completely disagree! I say thank you for everything I have learned, thank you for all the blessings provided, and thank you for being a hard year with a bunch of lessons on life. You have made me a better person and a stronger woman of faith.

James 1:2-4

> *Consider it pure joy, my brothers, whenever you face trials of many kinds, because you know that the testing of your faith develops perseverance. Perseverance must finish its work so that you may be mature and complete, not lacking anything.*

To the new year, I vowed to welcome it with open arms and readiness. A new year of lessons, a new year of memories, a new year full of victories! I was excited to see what the new year would hold for me and my family.

Psalm 20:4

May he give you the desire of your heart and make all your plans succeed.

Chapter Thirty-two
Last Couple of Weeks!

CaringBridge Entry
January 31, 2015

My church has just completed a two-week fast. I sat in church listening to our pastor speak on breakthroughs, clarity possibly happening, and listening and hearing what God has to speak to us in those two weeks.

I will be honest, I questioned it all. I feel connected, I feel my faith is also strong; what else could I learn from this, and what might I hear? So here is how the last two weeks have been.

My first day was the day we took Bentli on a tour of the College of Idaho, no big deal except they treated us to lunch. Yep, I was only having water that day.

As we walked into the biggest spread of food, Doug said, "Start tomorrow."

Bentli followed up with, "Mom, we won't tell anyone you ate!"

I sat with only my glass of water at lunch while everyone ate! Sacrifice. That is what I felt I was doing. I needed to learn sacrifice in these two weeks, and by starting the next day, or eating and not

125

telling anyone, I was not teaching myself anything. For I had lessons to learn.

My two-week fast went well. The first three days included water and a powder of energy food (from the wellness clinic). The next three days, I had only fresh juice. The last week, I ate veggies, fruits, and a little chicken. Never once did I feel I was starving, though at one point, I wanted to chew something.

I feel a clarity I have not had for a long time. It is like a bit of weight lifted off me. I guess you could say a cleansing of some sort. I sat in prayer, starting off with, "*guide me through this*," then as I sat in silence, it was more *guide yourself*. I believe yes, God guides us and helps us, but at that moment He was telling me to guide myself, trust myself. I think I had lost a little of that. Now, it's been regained! I regained the trust in myself.

In those two weeks, I was reminded again that we are *not* in charge. God is in charge, and when our lessons here on earth are complete, we are blessed with being welcomed home.

I feel this fast has inspired me to continue doing my work I need to be doing. When I get strung to the end of my rope, I know I have a Savior that will hold me until I climb back to the top. It has strengthened my soul to believe we are a blessing to many and a foundation for our little ones. It has reminded me that family is always first, ALWAYS! It has shown me that I can be in control, and I can do all things with the Lord right by my side. I am grateful for these past two weeks; it has opened my eyes to be faithful, loving, supportive, caring, and willing to do whatever is needed.

Doug's chemo treatments have been going really well. He seems to have no sickness—a bit of fatigue but nothing extreme. We are anxious for this next MRI; it seems the closer it gets to the appointment, the quieter we both get.

Doug looks really good. His numbers have been excellent, and he feels strong. He has been running open gym for softball at the high school and enjoying every minute of it.

It seems appropriate, as we get closer to the one-year mark, to write a letter.

Dear Adversity,

I first would like to thank you for coming into my life. I know that seems completely crazy, but because of you, I have become a new person. It seems you have taught me to fight, fight like I have never fought before. Because of you, I have a deeper love for life, my husband, my kids, my family, and my friends. I have been allowed to share my faith with many, which has helped me to keep you in check.

Having you in my life has given me strength that I did not think I had. I have been empowered by the experiences I have had in dealing with you. Thank you.

It seems you have joined our family in the last year, but within the last month, you have struck all three of my beauties. You really don't want to mess with this momma bear. But since you have come to them, I want you to know, YOU WILL NOT WIN! I have been by their sides guiding them through this. You have only allowed me to help them see how important Christ is in their lives and how sticking together, fighting, and supporting each other has only strengthened our family bond. Each beauty has been dealt her own adversity, and I will tell you, what that has done is made them stronger than they were before. Because of you, I know my beauties will be strong, confident, loving women of faith.

I would be so happy if you could give all of us a break. You have filled our lives for the last eleven months and we could use a vacation from you.

Thank you, Jacki

I think the hardest thing with adversity is we need to allow God to guide us and listen to where we need to be. We must understand that it may not be what we would choose but believe He has our best interest. I am believing and standing firm in my faith that what we have traveled is helping us to get to where we need to be and that there will be huge victories to scream about. Giving glory to God for them all. I am believing my husband is healed!

Psalm 28:7-8

The Lord is my strength and my shield; my heart trusts in him, and I am helped. My heart leaps for joy and I will give thanks to him in song. The Lord is the strength of his people, a fortress of salvation for his anointed one.

We got done with Doug's MRI. Anticipating the doctor to walk into that same small patient room we continue to find ourselves sitting in, I could feel the tension building. The slow cracking of the door had butterflies fill my stomach. I was concerned Doug would not be able to take another jab of bad news.

Then she entered. "How are you guys?"

I was quick to answer, "Good."

She looked at Doug. "How are you doing, Doug? How is your energy level?"

"I am doing pretty good," he responded quietly.

As she began to pull up the pictures of the MRI she stated, "There seems to be no measurable growth to the tumor."

With a look of confusion, I said, "There is no growth?"

"You are correct, the tumor is stable," she reassured. "Keep doing whatever you are doing."

TUMOR IS STABLE! Amen Jesus!

We are screaming with joy! Giving all glory to God on this amazing report!

Doug began to cry. I held him in my arms and asked if he was okay.

He said, "Yes, happy tears, Jack, happy tears!"

We must remember this is a very aggressive tumor, and the smallest of microscopic cells can possibly grow. We are believing this will not happen. This huge VICTORY we got is all credit to the good Lord above. Thank you, Jesus, for hearing our prayers. Through Him, all things are possible.

It has been a journey to be on, but at all times, I have held onto my faith and the belief He would answer prayers in due time. I am holding steadfast in my faith and believing. My prayers will continue for complete healing for my husband.

Matthew 21:22

If you believe, you will receive whatever you ask for in prayer.

I am thankful for the amazing doctors in Seattle and Boise. I am thankful to all the Team Corta warriors that have held us in prayer. But I am so thankful for the most amazing God that answers prayers and gives us guidance. Giving the glory to Him today!

Chapter Thirty-three

Study... Oh My!

Doug was invited to be a part of a study; he was a good candidate.

It was the first stage of the study; it had only been performed on dogs and rats. Ten candidates were asked to do this study.

Doug said to me, "Jack, if this can possibly help me and help others in the future, I want to do it."

His words truly touched my heart. Doug had to wear a headband that had a cord that was plugged into a small device that put frequency waves to his brain. They were hoping the frequency waves disrupted the tumor cells, keeping them from dividing and producing growth.

He'd need to stay in Seattle for seven days!

Wait, seven days?

Doug and I sat down and seriously talked about this. "Jack, we need to figure out how we are going to make this work."

"Douglas, we need to think about leaving the girls for that long, and honestly I need to be home working." I could see concern fill his face as I toyed with the idea of not going with him.

Silence filled the room for a minute. "Who would go with me, Jack? How could I go without you? Are you going to be okay not being in Seattle?"

As hard as it was to muster up the words, I replied, "Douglas, I am not sure if I will be okay not being there with you, but I also know our girls have sacrificed so much already with both of us being gone. Plus, I really need to be home so I can work."

He looked out the window and back at me with tears starting to build, "You are right Jack, as much as I want you there you need to be home."

That was a difficult decision for both of us since we'd been side by side for the last eleven months.

My mom traveled with him to Seattle. Being away from each other for seven days proved to be a challenge, but one we were willing to take in hopes that the study would be a breakthrough for GBM tumors.

As we prepared for his trip, we had our moments of tears. I think both of us were anxious about being away from each other. I know it sounds a bit crazy, or maybe a bit controlling on my part, but I felt our togetherness was part of what was keeping us sane.

One day while apart, I received the best text from Doug. He said, "I heard this song, and it was everything I would say to you. Please listen to it. I love you!"

I sat and bawled my eyes out as I listened to Tim McGraw's "My Best Friend."

I am one lucky lady to have such an amazing man in my life.

We had a love story for the record books. God knew what he was doing back when I was fifteen and this older guy walked into my life. I felt blessed to be traveling this journey called life with him by my side.

I found out Doug was the FIRST HUMAN IN THE WORLD to have the headband on and running. He completely embraced that step of our journey, but I found those seven days to be a challenge. My heart ached as I awaited his return!

Psalms 61:2

From the ends of the earth I call to you, I call as my heart grows faint; lead me to the rock that is higher than I.

Chapter Thirty-four
Love Story

Valentine's Day was usually just another day for Doug and me. Nothing special. I had always told him I didn't like going out on this day, there were always too many people. Restaurants are packed, movie theaters are full. I always told him, "Don't get me flowers, they die way too fast; it's a waste of money!"

That year was a bit different for me, a bit harder; my Valentine was in Seattle away from me.

As I looked at all the posts on Facebook and Instagram, the beautiful bouquets of flowers from loved ones, amazing date nights, coffee with that special one, hikes to the top of hills, creative gifts from little ones, and awesome gifts of jewelry, spa treatments, and fun getaways, I was brought to tears. My heart hurt.

I would not be wrapping my arms around my Valentine, no kisses, no hugs, not a card or a bouquet of flowers from him.

This was not a pity party because I was quickly reminded that in four days I would be getting to kiss, hug, hold, smell, and kiss some more of my sweet, sweet love.

I was awakened that morning by my phone ringing fairly early. As I grabbed my phone, I saw it was Doug calling. *Hmmmmm a bit early, I hope all is okay.* I clicked my answer button and said, "Hey, Babe!"

"Sorry to wake you so early," he started. I waited to detect urgency.

"It's fine, are you okay?"

"I couldn't sleep, I have been up since 2:00 A.M... Jack, I am tired, tired of everything." Hearing those words made me momentarily afraid. *What does this mean?*

Brushing away thoughts that were not in alignment with our mission of a fight, I recovered. "Babe, we are in this for the long haul. Douglas, you are all worked up over things you cannot control, or change. You need to stop letting the fear of things you cannot control run your thoughts. Will you please go take some calcium gluconate? It will help you relax."

I heard crying on the other end of the phone.

"Douglas," I continued, "I truly believe a lot of this is the fact we have been apart from each other." I hoped it was enough to start to quell his fear.

Doug acknowledged a very soft, "Yeah."

"Babe, we are on this journey together, the Lord has big plans for us. We are not stopping. We are fighting and going to do whatever we need to do, and we need to believe He will be with us every step of the way."

A sniffle came from his end. I waited patiently for words.

"Douglas are you okay?" Still nothing.

A long pause...

"Douglas!" I stated with an urgency that I'm certain startled him.

"I am okay." His whisper tugged at my heart.

I responded with the only thing I was certain of, the only thing that without a doubt was 100 percent true, "Sweets, I miss you!"

"I miss you, too, Jack, a lot." Whether my words actually helped him or if he just wanted me to feel better, we'd agreed.

That is where I wanted to just cry. I wanted to just give in to the tears, the exhaustion, the pain of this whole journey. But this was not the time for me to shed tears as I knew it would only work him up. We had many moments together where we both cried, and I knew the distance and my sobs would upset him. I pulled myself together, fastened my armor, and put my strongest face on.

"Jack, I am so sorry."

"For what?"

He replied, "For everything I am putting you through." We'd had that conversation many times before, but he needed the reassurance.

"Oh, sweets, you are not putting me through anything that I didn't choose to go through with you," was my heartfelt reply.

More sniffles and a long pause.

"Douglas, I love your guts, you mean more to me than you'll ever know. This journey called life we are doing, well, I am grateful to be doing it with you. God knows what He is doing with us. He, above all things, loves us and knows exactly where we are supposed to be."

"Yeah." He acquiesced. I was uncertain if he really meant he agreed or if he just hoped to soothe me.

"And right now, sweets, He needs you in Seattle and me in Idaho." I responded in that matter-of-fact way, the get-this-done sort of way that I'd learned was my way of holding the family together in strength.

"I guess. Jack…," he said, with a slight pause.

"Yeah, what babe?" *Do I really want to know why the pause?*

A much longer pause, "… I love you so much, you know I love you."

"Yes babe, I know you love me, but not as much as I love you."

I was fifteen years old when I told Doug I loved him for the first time. Trust me, I will never forget it because the night I said it, he looked at me and said, "Thanks!"

We had joked about it forever.

I knew at fifteen there was something about this love story, for the Lord kept taking me back to Doug. I didn't think I could love him more than I loved him the day I said the words for the first time. I was proven wrong; my love for him grew to be bigger than I could have ever imagined.

I am the first to say, it took cancer to make me realize how much I loved this guy. It took cancer to open my eyes to a love story I had no idea I was writing. It took cancer for me to say *I love cancer,* for what cancer has shown me, taught me, provided me, and continued to give to me!

——————

From that day, I began writing as much as I could. I believed God knew what He was doing in a very young fifteen-year-old when she prayed for Him to guide her to the one she was supposed to be with. He knew there would be a love story to be told, one that would include the love of the Lord, the blessings of His miracles, the power of prayer, the joy of His forgiveness, and the glory of the good fight.

2 Corinthians 9:6-8

> *Remember this: Whoever sows sparingly will also reap sparingly, and whoever sows generously will also reap generously. Each man should give what he has decided in his heart to give, not reluctantly or under compulsion, for God loves a cheerful giver. And God is able to make all grace abound to you, so that in all things at all times, having all that you need, you will abound in every good work.*

Chapter Thirty-five

Still Stable!

CaringBridge Entry
March 10, 2015

I have a routine going into the appointment to get the results of Doug's MRI. We walk from the waiting area to that small patient room holding hands. Sometimes our hands are more sweaty than other times. We sit down and I begin praying in my head.

Doug seems to be more quiet than usual, waiting, so I take that opportunity to pray. As soon as the doctor walks in, I start screaming in my head, *No growth! No growth!* I usually stop screaming once she says, "How are you guys?"

Doug was quick to respond this time, "Good."

"How was the trip over?"

"Uneventful, which is nice," I said. I wanted the results, not small talk.

She spun her stool toward Doug and said, "The tumor is still stable!"

A smile appeared on his face as the heaviness that filled my stomach left.

We are feeling very blessed. God is so good! We are trusting in Him and screaming this victory in His name! He, my God, gets ALL the glory! Getting out of the appointment, we busy ourselves with phone calls and text messages to let all the family know the news.

The girls have been doing really well lately, feeding off their dad for sure. It has been a relief to have a stable tumor, giving so much hope in those three young lives.

Psalms 20:7

Some trust in chariots and some in horses, but we trust in the name of the Lord our God.

Chapter Thirty-six

Great Weekend!

We had such a blast last weekend with our girl, Z, home and playing in the softball tournament.

I cooked dinner for the whole Weber State softball team and coaching staff. It was such a joy to be able to do it for them. I personally thanked them for the amazing support they gave Z and our family.

These young ladies have learned more about life than they even know, through softball. A family, that is what they have built. In my eyes, that is bigger than any game they will ever play. I love those girls and each of their fearless leaders they call Coach.

People always hope that when their kids grow up, they will end up in a good place, somewhere they will be able to grow as individuals and make lifelong friendships. This is exactly what Z did at Weber State. I could not have handpicked a better place for her to have been, or better friends than she made.

It is interesting how we don't see God working until the work is almost complete. When Z got back from her visit at Weber State, she said to me, "Mom, this is where I am supposed to be. I could feel it when I walked on the field and as I walked the campus. Even if I don't get a scholarship, this is where I am supposed to be."

I brushed her off and said I am glad the visit went well, and we should wait to see what they offered her. Looking back, I now believe it was a God thing getting her to Weber State. She was offered a scholarship in the fall. I am thankful she listened to her calling and thankful for the love of the amazing role models she had as coaches. God always has a plan; we sometimes don't know it right away.

I am always taken aback when I can actually see the Lord working right in front of me. I do believe we sometimes get too busy in our daily lives. We forget to slow down to see Him work. But on one trip, it was quite apparent He was working right in front of me.

On our visit to Seattle, I went to get in line to get Doug and me water. As I approached the end of the line, a handsome, older gentlemen approached me as if he knew me and said, "Hi, how are you?" He then went on to say, "It's a beautiful day, isn't it?"

"Yes, the sunshine is amazing."

At this point a young lady walked up and asked if we were both in line. The gentleman quickly said no as I was about to say yes.

I told the lady to go ahead. I felt like I needed to stay and visit more with him. He put his hand on my shoulder and said to me, "Don't forget to always see the sunshine, wherever you may be." He looked deep into my eyes and continued, "Life is so much better when we can see the light even when we think it is dark. You are doing good and today will be fine." He tapped my shoulder again and said, "I am not exactly sure why you are here but keep being well."

I was in shock at what I was hearing. I told him to have a nice day, and I stepped to the line. I felt drawn to still visit with him, but as I turned around, he was gone. *GONE!* I could not see him outside the door, or down the hall next to the coffee shop.

As I sat back down with Doug, I told him about the most amazing encounter with a stranger. Again, I believe it was the Lord working right in front of me. I was very anxious to get the results of Doug's MRI, and this stranger brought me peace.

In our everyday lives, we are on fast mode for most of the day, and we are not going to see the simple blessings the Lord has for us. We need to find a moment to walk at a slower pace and see what we are missing when we are speed walking through life. The job, the computer, the phone, the TV, the emails will not bring us the joy of listening whole heartedly to our children telling us about their day. It's time to slow down.

Lamentations 3:22-23

Because of the Lord's great love we are not consumed, for his compassions never fail. They are new every morning; great is your faith-fulness.

Chapter Thirty-seven

Happy One-Year Anniversary!

CaringBridge Entry
March 13, 2015

March 13th will forever be etched in my soul. This is the day that my whole world turned upside down. I can replay that whole day in my head like it was yesterday.

And yet, in this last year, I have seen amazing changes happen at my house. I have watched three girls grow up very fast. I have seen them hear the most horrific news children could possibly hear and become completely weak and beyond scared. I have witnessed them becoming stronger—stronger young ladies within themselves and stronger in their faith. I have watched five people have a bond that seems unbreakable become even stronger.

I continue to watch the love of my life fight for his! I have seen him at his weakest, and I have watched him transform into a man of faith. I see blessing after blessing happening in the midst of a complete hurricane.

In the last year, I have learned more about life than I even knew was possible. I have watched amazing friends and complete strangers come forward to support and rally around us. I have witnessed a collegiate softball team of young ladies commit to supporting my girl and our family. I have learned on this journey how important each day really is, how we need to give thanks for every sunrise, sunset, and rainy day we get to have.

I have learned just because you have cancer or there is cancer in your life, mean people are still mean. I have learned a smile can go a long way. I have learned how to fake having a good day. I have learned my life is my journey with many lessons. I have learned to face adversity with my whole heart and to not allow it to take me down. I have learned it is okay to weep when needed but to not stay there. I am learning it is okay to ask for and to allow people to help.

In a year, I have learned life is too short to hold grudges, to not forgive, and to question the challenges we face. I found there is more beauty in the world when cancer joins the family.

I am so grateful to have cancer in my life because it has softened my heart and opened my eyes. It has shown me how strong I am and how it is also okay to be weak. I am grateful for cancer because it has made me a truer Jacki. I am true to who I am, and I am true to every single person in my life.

I am grateful for the lessons cancer has taught me. Some have been harder than others, but they were lessons that needed to be taught, lessons I needed to learn. I am grateful for cancer because it has given me a platform I can stand tall on and scream from the top of my lungs—proclaiming my beliefs, my views, my lessons, my trials, and my victories—a platform I hold very dear to my heart. One that when I step up on it and begin to share, I am always hoping one soul will be motivated, inspired, moved, or maybe their eyes will be opened, or their heart might be softened. It is a platform the Lord has given me to use.

James 1:12

*Blessed is the man who perseveres under trial,
because when he has stood the test, he will
receive the crown of life that God has promised
to those who love him.*

Chapter Thirty-eight

Happy Easter!

CaringBridge Entry
April 4, 2015

Softball season is in full swing!

Doug has had another round of chemo; this one was a bit tough. It made him sicker this time. The good news is he is completely enjoying coaching this season. He has a new outlook on how he is coaching, what he wants to accomplish as a coach, and he's figured out what is important to him as a coach.

This season is more about the girls than actual wins. He wants to show them strength and how to approach and handle challenges not only on the field but in life. If wins come with those goals, it is only more exciting. He has vocalized to me that he is planting seeds in these girls to have for the rest of their lives.

I am always reminded I am not in control, and that my Almighty God has the best interest for me in our journey. It becomes very hard sometimes with His decisions when I feel things should be one way, but He knows differently.

As we get ready to travel back to Seattle, my anxiety ratchets up. I do my best to keep holding on to the last two stable MRIs. Some days, I even find myself forgetting how serious Doug's diagnosis truly is.

He is strong, doing what he loves, coaching softball. He is active; he seems healthy! Then I remember how serious it is. That's the thing with hidden diseases like cancer, and why we should never judge people by how they look.

I watched about seven minutes of a sixty-minute story on GBM tumors and my heart couldn't take anymore. It spoke of the severity of the tumor and the short life span of the patients. Reality slapped me across my face.

I turned my focus and energy to prayer instead. I am choosing to believe in miracles and in more victories, believing that through this trial we are facing, lessons are being learned, hearts are being softened, and lives are being transformed.

If you are experiencing your own trials, having your own disbeliefs, or maybe doors are being shut for you, with a tear in my eye, I say to you, *it does suck*; it truly feels as if you are sinking sometimes, but you have a choice. You can allow yourselves to fall victim to all of it or you can pull yourselves up and stand against the dark. And if you don't have enough energy to get up on your own, you can look up, reach to the sky, and allow the Lord to hold you until you can stand on your own. You can choose to see the good that is coming from your trial.

I have seen lives being changed with our story. Souls are finding happiness in their own way. Outlooks on things are now being seen with clarity. We have witnessed those bringing their faith back. Through our choices on how we are living out *our* story, we are impacting more than we ever knew.

In a one-year span, my husband was diagnosed with an incurable GBM tumor, with an average of fifteen months survival. It's the get-your-things-in-order-and-start-your-goodbyes kind of brain cancer. And since the entire tumor wasn't removed, starting radiation and chemo hopefully prolonged the survival time a bit.

Doug started his fight, and I started my new life. One I really wasn't prepared for.

While I'm tending to my recovering husband and my three girls, I'm also running two businesses, one that I had no clue how to run. I went from working two days a week, enjoying some me time, to working six days a week, and dealing with unhappy and happy employees, unhappy customers, and an unhappy me.

We can face challenges in our lives, and we can fight the good fight, but we can also be extremely unhappy we are having to do it. Because I find myself so busy with everything and everyone else, I have lost a bit of my identity—at least the identity I had before this.

Choosing to stay unhappy is how we can get ourselves in trouble or sick. I have allowed myself to feel these emotions, partly because they are normal and need to be felt. Then I choose to rally myself back to the front line of this fight.

My point with all of this is, I could have stopped at the first doctor's appointment when he told us how serious the diagnosis was. I could have given up, sat with Doug, and said our goodbyes. But instead, the first thing out of my mouth to the neurosurgeon was, "NOW WE FIGHT!"

I look back now and believe he thought I was in complete denial of what I had heard. But there was something that came over me that was like, *Jack, you are going to fight, you are going to not only touch people, but you are going to change people.*

Now, let's talk about the good in this last year. My faith grew so much my heart feels as if it could burst. I have witnessed an army of friends, family, and strangers rally around us. I have had the pleasure of meeting the most amazing doctors in the Northwest. I watched my husband put Christ back in his life and put Him in the front of the line.

I have become a true person myself; I am who you get. I will forever be true to who I am.

There has been a team of young ladies supporting my daughter while away and learning a few things about how precious life is. I have watched my husband soften and truly see what life is really about—what life truly means to him. And on top of it all, I am choosing every day to make it a better day.

Now don't get me wrong, there are plenty of really bad days. I find myself in tears and not wanting to continue the fight or feeling I don't have the bandwidth to continue the fight and keep my household and businesses going. But those are the days I rely on my faith, my family, my friends, and yep, sometimes it is the stranger that smiled at me. But it has been my choice from the start that I would fight, and I would not let a GBM tumor rule my life.

For someone new on this journey, don't allow yourself to be shackled to your trials. You can be sad and frustrated, but only for a moment. Choose to see the good in your trial. Choose now to fight. Adversity is going to strike everyone; it is how you react to that adversity that will define you.

So, if you are that one soul that I felt I needed to reach, know you are loved, you are going to be okay, know you are a fighter, and you have so much good around you. Take a minute and look around. Always, always, always BELIEVE!

James 1:6

> *But when he asks, he must believe and not doubt,*
> *because he who doubts is like a wave of the sea,*
> *blown and tossed by the wind.*

With another quick trip to Seattle for a routine MRI, I seem to be unable to get rid of the anxiety today. But at least at this appointment, I didn't have to wait long for the result.

As we sat in that small patient room again, Doug and I had a conversation. This is usually when we both are very quiet. But this day we talked about the girls, how softball was going, and what we needed to do when we got back home.

In walks the doctor, "MRI shows the tumor is stable."

She didn't even give me time to develop the yucky pit in my stomach. She didn't even ask how we were. I was grateful. Grateful for the quickness of the results. *Prayers are being answered!* We are yelling at the top of our lungs, "GOD IS GOOD!"

TUMOR IS STILL STABLE!

Psalm 118:24

This is the day the Lord has made; let us rejoice and be glad in it.

Chapter Thirty-nine
Treatment Plan

We went and watched Z and her Weber State team win the Big Sky Tournament, qualifying them for the NCAA Regionals! The selection show announced they are headed to Louisiana to play! How incredible it was to know our girl had dreamed of this since she was little and would get to experience it. We were so excited for her.

I told her to take in every moment, enjoy it, have fun, and take lots of photos! With Doug and the girls still in season, my needing to work and Doug's health, we could not travel to Louisiana, unfortunately.

Doug finished his regular season undefeated. Wow, what a huge accomplishment. His softball team was on our local news station on *Sunday Sports Extra*. It was really fun to see them, but I loved watching the smile on Doug's face as "his" girls were all up there being shown off.

The KTVB sports director did an amazing piece on Doug and his assistant coach from last year. They were both battling cancer. It was a beautiful piece that reached many. We were very pleased with how well he told our story, and the story of the softball team, and what adversity they had been through.

Doug's team made it all the way to the finals, and they won! It was his first state championship!

It was a group of fourteen- to eighteen-year-old girls that, without a doubt in my mind, experienced more adversity than any team in the state. Their head coach having brain cancer and their interim assistant coach being diagnosed with breast cancer, combined with the normal trials of being a high schooler—*adversity* almost seems an inadequate word.

These girls reminded me how to fight, how to not settle, how to love, how to support, and how to be a TEAM. They, without even knowing it, have been etched into my heart FOREVER! This bunch of young ladies will forever be remembered for overcoming and fighting through adversity and for being the best support to their coach, even when they had no idea they were supporting him.

This team learned about softball their whole life, and in one year, they learned a lot more about the game of life. I could not be prouder of each and every one of those girls.

THANK YOU! THANK YOU! THANK YOU for putting a smile on Doug's face every single day, for making him giggle, for giving him what he needed, for understanding when he couldn't be there, for supporting him in the shadows, for being more than just an athlete on a team. I will always love your guts, and I am beyond proud of what you girls accomplished!

Doug was named coach of the year for 5A SIC. Being back on the field that year was a huge blessing in our house. Seeing him doing what he was so passionate about and loving every minute of it truly impacted me. It was in the simple things people couldn't see or hear from him that I most enjoyed. When he came home from practice and told me the littlest things a player did, he talked with a smile on his face as if he were talking about his own daughter.

———

CaringBridge Entry
May 18, 2015

After Doug's latest MRI, the doctor walked in and went right into "How are you feeling, how are things going, are you having headaches?"

She did some neurological testing on Doug and then said, "The MRI does not look good. There are three spots of growth." She didn't slow her talk down and continued with, "Nothing seems to be working, we need to look at other options." And she still didn't slow down. She suddenly spoke about Doug's quality of life. It seems really good right now, but with these aggressive tumors, that can diminish quickly, and when that happens, we will look into hospice!

WAIT A MINUTE. Why are we even saying the "H" word right now?

I looked up at Doug; he was deflated. She took all life he had right out of him with that one word. He looked at me with more fear than I have ever seen in his eyes.

He looked at the doctor and said, "Are you saying I have years?"

"No."

He then said, "Days?"

She said, "No, no, not days."

I wanted him to stop asking, and I wanted her to stop talking. I sat there quietly.

She then said, "I can give you my clinical overview of a timeline if you want."

Doug softly said, "I am scared to hear it." He began to cry.

We moved on to talking about the next CyberKnife radiation treatment. *Thank you, God, I did not want to hear a number.* She gave us both a hug and said we would have another MRI in eight weeks. Our neurosurgeon then entered the room and seemed upset with the findings.

Doug began to cry; the doctor walked over and hugged him tightly.

Doug, through tears began, "I'm going to miss everything. I won't see Demi graduate; I won't walk any of my girls down the aisle on one of the most exciting days of their lives; I will never know what it's like to hold my own grandkids. I can't believe this is happening to me!"

Barely keeping it together, I kept telling him we needed to stay strong. Then I decided. Today, today we will let this be ugly. We went to the cafeteria to get something to eat before we got on the road home.

We were sitting there eating, and Doug softly said to me, "I hope this goes fast."

I said, "What did you say?"

He began to cry and said, "I hope this goes fast, for you."

We both began to cry. I said, "Please, don't say that."

"Jack, I have never wanted to hurt you."

"Sweets, I signed up for this. You are not hurting me." *Is it the truth?* Yes, I was hurting. But it most definitely was not him hurting me!

With the sincerest look in his eyes, he said, "I am so lucky to have you."

I responded, "I am pretty lucky to have you, and I love you so much." I followed it with, "NOW WE FIGHT! WE CONTINUE TO FIGHT!"

On the road we went.

New plan: Doug will have ten treatments of CyberKnife radiation. There is a 5 percent chance of permanent side effects including seizures, headaches, or increased intracranial pressure. I am standing firm that this won't happen.

Doug is very scared and concerned.

I am believing and standing firm in complete healing. I know we are on a journey; I know we don't know the outcome, but I do know if I allow the Lord to guide us and give us strength and allow Him to do His work, all things are possible; ALL THINGS ARE POSSIBLE.

I said to Doug today, as he is still struggling, that we can bend, but we will not break! We will not let the noise of the enemy ring in our heads. We will focus on the ever-loving guidance from our God, our Almighty God!

Chapter Forty

Headed Home

We flew in Thursday morning with his first treatment that afternoon. As we walked in, I felt the shift happening in Doug. He began to get very quiet and a bit agitated. I sat rubbing his back saying a blessing over him hoping for some sort of peace.

A young couple walked in, and I always found myself wondering what other people's stories were.

The nurse walked out with a sweet woman, probably in her sixties, who said, "Oh, there's my daughter."

They walked toward her, and the daughter said, "How was it?"

She replied, "I was so grateful. I lay there thinking I am so grateful. So grateful to be able to be here, and so grateful for such an amazing machine. I kept thinking, I am so grateful."

Her son-in law asked her if she listened to any music, and she replied, "Yes, the piano, it was beautiful."

That woman had the most precious smile. She looked over at Doug and me, and I stood up and said, "I feel like I need to give you a hug!"

She accepted it kindly saying, "Honey, do you have family back there?"

I pointed at Doug and said he was about to go into his treatment. I sat back down next to Doug; she asked him if it was his first treatment.

He explained it was for this round, but he'd had CyberKnife radiation treatment before.

By that time, she stood directly in front of Doug. She grabbed his hands and stated, "We got this!" She asked his name and then said, "I'm Dr. Pete!" Then she followed it with, "You know we got this!" She put her palms together up against her lips, I thought maybe she was going to pray. She bent forward toward Doug and said, "BE BLESSED!"

He replied, "Thank you, bless your heart."

They walked out the door.

Doug turned to me and said, "Now, I'm ready, Jack!" A stillness came over him.

I leaned in and said, "Isn't it great how the Lord puts people in our path at the exact moment we need them?"

He smiled and said, "Yes."

The nurse came out and took Doug back. I went upstairs, and while in line at Starbucks, Dr. Pete approached. She asked how Doug was, and I told her she had been a huge blessing for him today.

She grabbed my hands and told me, "Your hug, honey, was very powerful; it really had something I needed. You are so sweet."

I thanked her and said to enjoy her afternoon. I love how our God made great things happen even at trying times. He is always near, for I was praying peace for Doug and out walks Dr. Pete. Wow, God is good!

The girls came to Seattle the evening of day three of treatment. Dinner as a family and walking the pier made for a great ending to that day. Day four of treatment was early in the morning, then we rolled everyone out of bed for breakfast and off to downtown and Pike's Market.

We enjoyed strolling around Seattle, in no hurry, embracing the time together. We, of course, watched fish fly and saw the famous gum wall. We had lunch back in our rooms and a short nap for Doug, then we were off to the Mariner's game. We surprised the girls with tickets in the fourth row from the field on the first base side.

The joy on Doug's face watching his girls have so much fun made the trip for me! Two balls caught—both signed—a beautiful night! We even had two appearances on the jumbotron! Rally hats on and Mariner Dogs! So much joy filled this momma. In the moments of distress, I knew it was important to find the joy of little things.

Day five was the last treatment, then we headed back to Idaho.

On our way home from Seattle, we enjoyed a bit of rest and spent some much-needed time at my sister's house in Halfway, Oregon. The beauty out her backdoor was exactly what my soul needed to soak up.

Doug had chemo in Boise on Tuesday and then we returned to Seattle for his next three treatments.

Z joined us on this trip because I needed an extra driver to get us home Friday night because we had a big weekend with Bentli graduating on Saturday and her party on Sunday.

Doug handled the radiation and seemed to only have some fatigue. We made it home safely Friday night as planned.

My house was cleaned, and the party organized and ready to go for Sunday. Saturday was filled with mixed emotions. We were so excited to be home again, but that lump in my throat was building. How could this be, how could my boo be graduating?

I was so proud of her for all she had endured the last year and a half. I had no time for tears. I barely had enough time to change the clothes out of our luggage to leave again for Seattle.

The graduation party was perfect. With a house still full of guests, Doug and I had to catch a flight back to Seattle for five days. My emotions had ramped up over the week prior—my girl graduating, my husband's treatments, my complete exhaustion, my worries of a mom leaving her girls, everything crashing altogether—and it all exploded.

As we were saying goodbye, the floodgates were opened, and the tears wouldn't stop. Off to the airport we went. Doug and I returned Friday, finally home for five weeks before he had to go back for another MRI. We both were beyond happy to walk into our house and sit on our deck.

Saturday was filled with a busy day of clients in the salon. My mom called and said she had not been feeling well but thought it would pass or she might go to the doctor on Monday.

Sunday, as we were headed to church, Mom sent me a text: "What time do you get out of church?"

I responded, "At 11:45, why?"

She replied, "Curious."

I didn't think twice about it. Off to church we went. As we were walking out of church, I saw I had a text from Mom.

"So you know: I am at the Urgent Care in Eagle."

I immediately called her, and she said the pain in her stomach region was extremely bad. We headed straight there. As we were walking in, she was coming out, barely able to walk. The nurse said she needed to go to the ER and have a CT scan.

Off to St. Luke's ER we went. The doctor came in and said, "We are going to do labs and a CT scan to check for appendicitis, gallbladder, or kidney stones."

Z and I sat with Mom; my aunt was kind enough to come sit with Dad in the waiting area.

After the CT scan, the doctor came in and said, "Well, you have appendicitis. You will have surgery in about three to six hours."

Phew, appendicitis. Take it out, recover, and Mom is good to go. Dad and my aunt walked in. Z and I went outside, I told them to take notes. That is where the Lord was working for me.

Z went to get sandwiches, and I made phone calls to my sisters. As I was walking back in, the nurse came out and got me. She said the doctor is with Mom and wanted me to join them.

That was my first clue. I pulled the curtain back to walk in and my mom was crying. In my head I am thinking *what is going on?*

The doctor said, "I have some bad news."

I looked down at my aunt, she gave me the stern eyes, as if it would be okay. He continued, "Your mom does have appendicitis and will have surgery today, but in the CT scan, it also showed a cancerous mass on one of her kidneys."

That's where my stone-cold face engaged, and the warrior came out.

I looked him in the face, saying, "Okay, so can you remove the kidney when you remove the appendix?"

He said, "No. Different doctors. Different teams."

I looked over at Mom, tears streaming down her face. He told us the urologist would be there the next day to visit with us about the plan for the kidney. But it was suspicious of renal cell carcinoma.

Well, I didn't know what that meant, but it didn't sound good. *Cancer? Cancer? CANCER! I am so sick of that word!*

He said to me, "I am so sorry." I reached over and grabbed Mom's leg, and as I walked out of the room, I stated, "Well, this is where we KEEP FIGHTING THE FIGHT!"

I went outside to call my sisters, Jodi and Cindi. Shock, maybe shock was what I felt. Disbelief. *How could this be happening again?* Anger, yeah maybe I was feeling anger. I sat on a bench, made a few more phone calls, asked a few of my prayer warriors to start praying.

Another uncle and aunt showed up, and when Z got back from getting sandwiches, I told her.

She looked at me and said, "Mom, what is going on? Why us again?"

No answer. I had no answer. I called Bentli and told her what was going on, and I got complete silence on the other end. I told her to bring Dad to the hospital to meet us. Grammy was about to go into surgery, and I wanted to tell Doug in person. He had latched onto my mom, and I was afraid of what this news might do to him. He was barely back to finding his own fight.

They got to the hospital, and he walked up to me and asked how I was doing.

I said, "I am good, but I need to tell you something." Fast and quick, I blurted it out and didn't give him any time to interrupt.

He looked at me, and I said, "In the CT scan they found a cancerous mass on her kidney; the doctor will be here tomorrow to discuss it with us."

He leaned down and kissed me and whispered, "It's not, and it's going to be okay!"

I said, "Yep, it is going to be okay."

We all sat and waited for the surgeon to come out. Jodi got there before Mom went in and Cindi was on her way. Surgery was about thirty-five minutes. He said she did good and would be up to her room in an hour.

She was a bit drowsy when she got to her room, but we all piled in.

Doug sat down next to her bed, and said, "Hi Grammy, you did good."

She smiled.

He followed it with, "I brought you my blanket, so you can use it."

I began to cry; in fact, I ran out of the room and straight to the elevator. The damn thing would not open fast enough, I needed air, and I needed it right then! My aunts caught me, and we headed down. I was done. I cried and screamed, "I can't do anymore, I can't do anymore! My legs are weak, and I am done!"

The fresh air felt good, even though it was ridiculously hot. I had to plan who would stay with Mom and who would stay with Dad. Doug had chemo in the morning, so I needed to be with him. We got it all worked out.

The urologist came in that night and showed us the CT scan of the tumor, and he brought us so much comfort. He said it would be surgically removed and then there would be no chemo or radiation. His exact words, "We remove it, you are down for two weeks and then back to living the rest of your life." She needed to recover from the first surgery before they would do the next.

Doug had chemo on Monday, and Mom was released from the hospital. On Wednesday morning, as Doug and I sat on our deck having coffee, my phone rang. It was Mary from the Nativis study in Seattle that Doug was in.

She told me they had decided to allow Doug to re-enroll into the study. YAHOOOO! Doug was really excited. When he had the last MRI done and it showed growth, that immediately defaulted the trial, and he no longer could be part of it. So, getting this message that he could re-enroll was amazing.

I said, "Great will you mail us the headbands?"

She said, "No, that is the not-so-good news. This is like he has never been enrolled, so we have to start from the beginning. We have him scheduled for an MRI on Tuesday and his eight-day visit on Monday."

"WAIT. Do we have to stay seven days again?" I almost couldn't process this. I didn't know how to ride this part of the wave.

She said, "No, you can go home, but he has to be back on the eighth day." Pure excitement turned into a full-on whirlwind again. Just when I thought we would be home for five weeks straight, we were, instead, headed back in three days. Oh, and then again, the next week. We were anxious to be back on the study, so that was great news. Doug truly felt better when he had his headband.

Frazzled was my new word. I felt a bit frazzled. My life seemed to be going a hundred miles an hour and I couldn't seem to catch up.

Our pastor gave a great message that Sunday, and something really stuck with me that he said…

"If you want your life message clearly heard, then you need to clearly listen!"

This means listening in silence, listening for guidance, listening for the sound of what you cannot hear.

In those three weeks I had been going and going and going, so that night, I sat and listened. Silence… silence… *be still*…

Hmmmmm, be still? That's what I hear, *be still*? Then, I was brought to:

Psalms 37:7

> *Be still before the Lord and wait patiently for him; do not fret when men succeed in their ways, when they carry out their wicked schemes.*

It made me recheck myself. I had had some really crappy days recently. Don't get me wrong, I had looked at myself in the mirror and told myself, "Yep this sucks right now, but girlfriend, you better decide what you want to do."

There were moments I wanted to sit in the corner and bawl my eyes out. There were moments I want to scream out of anger so the whole world could hear me. There were moments I was not sure I could keep going; there were moments, moments of silence, that said *be still*.

I always knew the Lord worked when we were unaware. It was a blessing my mom had appendicitis so we could find the tumor before it was too late.

My life message continued forward, I knew I would reach that one soul, that one soul who needed to hear my message. Today, today, be still!

Chapter Forty-one

So Much to Be Grateful for

Doug received a stable MRI; Mom had kidney surgery, and everything went really well. Mom's tumor was encapsulated; they removed it and got a clear reading of tissue around it. I felt a bit of relief and was taking every victory with grace.

I felt very consumed but continued to hold on to my faith and to trust in His plan. Even though there had been more thrown at me, I was willing to take it. There was a strength that had filled me that I can only believe came from the Lord above.

Although I had breakdowns and wasn't sure if I could carry any more, in those moments I felt His presence so strongly within me. It was a choice to keep moving forward and not let the things we are thrown, and must face, pull us down. We continued to choose.

Psalms 9:10

Those who know your name will trust in you, for you, Lord, have never forsaken those who seek you.

The definition of a caregiver (i.e., a person who provides direct care for children, elderly people, or the chronically ill) does not sit well with me; I believe there is so much more to it than that.

I was blessed with three babies. People choose this type of caregiving because we know going into it that we will be caring for our children. We try to prepare ourselves as best we can to be the best caregivers to them. We read the books, we might have even taken some parenting classes—*man, I should have taken those classes!* There was time to get our mindset ready. We made the changes that needed to be made in our lives to be fully ready. We even put people in place to help us. This type of caregiving, to me, is a privilege.

As we grew up, we also watched every move our parents were making. We saw how they were with their own parents, and as they aged, we were reminded that one day we could be caring for them.

We start out completely dependent on our parents, then it goes full circle to the point where they could one day be completely dependent on us.

My grandma and grandpa were amazing people. They had more unconditional love than I have ever seen. They raised eight kids on a farm, teaching them hard work and family values. As my grandparents began to age, I learned so much from my parents and aunts and uncles. What my grandparents instilled in their kids shone through each of them as they began having to care for their aging parents. Shifts were taken by each of them. Adult grandkids even took shifts. We learned from the best about caring for our family.

We had *time* to prepare ourselves, we had things in order for when the time came, and we were ready. For me, this type of caregiving is a no-brainer. Family is always first. We take care of those who have taken care of us. This is what a family does, and it is love.

It is the unexpected sickness or disability that can be a challenge. We are not prepared; the tools are not in place. The role of caregiver happens in a blink of an eye.

Someone asked me how I was doing, and I immediately started saying, "WE are good, Doug feels pretty good..."

They stopped me and said, "I asked how YOU are doing!"

That example shows, with this type of caregiving, we don't have much time to think of ourselves. It is a twenty-four seven job. You are caring for your loved one physically and mentally all the time. And when you are not doing that, you are constantly wondering about—and in many cases reading, studying, or researching—the illness, and that's on top of working and trying to keep a household going.

And then, you're also trying your best to keep life as normal as possible for your kids. There are moments when I wish I had an off button. A moment to have my old life back, the one before cancer came into it. I wish I could have a moment where cancer is not running through my head.

With this type of caregiving, you may be left wondering every moment what is coming next. *What will I run into around the next corner? What will be over the next mountain we climb?* When kids are part of the equation, you are constantly wondering how they are doing.

My wedding vows read, "through sickness and health unto death do us part." I stood at an altar in front of family, friends, and God, and I said those vows to Doug. Vows I cherish, vows that mean a commitment, vows that, if you read the fine print, might say in sickness, the *really bad* kind of sickness. The sickness that will throw you into a caregiver role.

There is not a choice in my mind. You wake up each morning and you keep putting one foot in front of the other. You become stronger than you ever thought you could be. You choose to be!

It is a blessing to be this type of caregiver. I was shown so many things when I assumed this role. Things I would say I wish I would have known without cancer teaching them to me. I truly am amazed how beautiful the flowers smell!

Before Doug's cancer, I rarely stopped to smell the flowers. There was always too much going on—places to be, people to see, with no slowing down on my part. I see things differently now.

Cancer actually put more joy in my life, strengthened my love for my husband, gave me more compassion towards my kids, and created a tighter bond with our family. I can honestly say, cancer made me fall in love with my husband all over again but at a deeper level. I gazed at him as if I was that teenage girl, giddy for his attention.

Before cancer, we had gotten comfortable in our ways. We'd been married for so many years; he did his thing, I did mine. He had his friends, I had mine, we had some together. He wanted this, I wanted that. Compromise seemed to go out the door.

Cancer pushed us together. When I was gone for the day and I returned home, I couldn't wait to put my arms around him. I couldn't wait to kiss him. I couldn't wait to be by him because there was that chance I wouldn't always have him there to do that.

We were married twenty-one years before cancer entered our life. Looking back, that was twenty-one years I now wish I would have truly embraced even more. I wish I'd truly loved on him every night. I wish I would not have cared how the towels were folded, or if the bread dried out, or if there was toothpaste in the cap.

I can say that with as much hurt cancer brought me that year, it also strengthened my marriage and taught me to see the joy in my life. It made me a stronger person.

CaringBridge Entry
August 2, 2015

So, to the sweet person who asked me that day how I was doing, here is my real answer:

I am okay. I am managing to the best of my ability with what has been put in front of me. I cry a lot. I cry a lot when I am alone. I have moments of extreme anger. I get very frustrated when I want a moment for me, and it is taken away because I have to take care of all the other stuff on my plate.

I have a lot of moments of sadness, mainly when my mind wanders, and I think of my sweet girls and what they are having to experience at such a young age. I have sadness seeing my best friend fight for his life and witnessing him having days when he doesn't want to fight anymore.

Those days are my hardest. I want to give him grace but also want to shout, "THERE IS NO TIME FOR GIVING UP!" When the days of him not wanting to fight happen, I find myself carrying the load and allowing him to rest.

Fighting this fight is exhausting and mentally tough on all of us. Honestly, there are days when it fills me with absolute fear because I know the outcome of this fight and feeling any slight submission to it could take Doug. Overcoming those days takes a lot of prayer and willingness on my part.

Ultimately, at any point, I could have fallen into defeat, but I choose to continue the battle we are facing. He rests and I pray. He wants to give up and I rebuke it in the name of Jesus. I remind us both of the reason we fight, and the number one reason is our three daughters.

I have learned some great coping mechanisms that get me through the day. But I rely on my life motto, which is tattooed on my arm: "It's All Good!" It really is, even when it is bad, it truly is still good.

Chapter Forty-two

Girls Off to College

Even though we got another stable MRI, the sendoff to college was a bit harder as the girls wanted to be home with their dad and me.

We were sitting in our living room when the girls made it known they wanted to stay home.

"I can take classes online," Z spoke.

"What about softball, Z?" Doug came back with.

"It is fine, I don't care, it is only fall ball."

Doug quickly said, "I do *not* want you missing softball. Mom and I will be fine."

Bent piped in, "I can take a gap year and be home with you guys."

Before she could even finish that sentence, Doug was shaking his head and firmly said, "No, you will *not* do that."

There was a moment of silence. Some mumbling from the girls, "Dad, it will be fine."

Again, Doug looked up at me, turned towards the girls and said, "You both need to go to school. That is where you need to be, and that is what I want you both doing: going to school and playing softball."

I could feel the heartache fill the room as they knew what Dad wanted but they wanted to be home. He wanted to keep things as normal as could be and that meant having them both back at school. I wonder now if it was his way of protecting them.

I assured them they would not be left out of the loop with Dad's health. They both could come home every weekend if needed. Both girls' college coaches had been so understanding with their situation and were so supportive and had allowed them the freedom to be home when needed, but it was pulling on heartstrings leaving their dad.

I can't say if insisting they go back to school was right, but Douglas and I knew how much the girls meant to him, and how much their teams meant to them. Softball was a teacher where he could not be. It was an extension of him in their daily lives in a way that even he did not recognize.

I would have loved to have them at home, but Doug's wishes came first, and I refused to put more pressure on him than he was already feeling.

———————

CaringBridge Entry
Late August

This type of cancer is ferocious, but I have done a good job not creating space for that.

Today we got the results of Doug's MRI. Even though we had a stable MRI last month, Doug's tumor has grown and has grown viciously. The latest MRI shows that the tumor has spread throughout the whole right side of his brain. It is inoperable. His left side is weak, and he is struggling to walk. We are waiting to hear from the oncologist on the course of action we take next.

We are heartbroken.

Yesterday we walked into the oncologist appointment before Doug's chemo treatment.

"Good morning you guys," the oncologist said.

"Good morning," Doug said quietly.

She promptly spoke, "Doug, things seem a bit weaker than last visit. I would like to hold off on chemo today and would like to do an MRI."

We had been told to always have the MRIs at the same location with the same machines. That would give us the most accurate readings. She could see my concern as I started to say, "In Seattle?"

"You would need to be in Seattle by tomorrow to get it," she continued. "Or you can have it done today here."

I looked at Doug for his response.

"Jack, I don't want to travel to Seattle. Let's do it here in Boise."

Flutters filled my insides as I could hear the very prominent concerns in her voice, along with Doug not wanting to make the trip to Seattle.

So, the MRI was done in Boise just a few hours after this appointment.

Last night I could see Doug was struggling with the fact he had to have another MRI so soon. So, I asked, "Douglas what's going on?"

He stared out our large picture window, as I gave him a moment to just be. "Jack, is this it…?"

I interrupted him, "Sweets, I have no idea what the MRI will show, but whatever it is, we are not letting it alter our fight. It is okay to be sad."

"I'm scared, Jack. I don't want the girls to live without a dad."

Tears flowed as I declared, "We are going to try to LIVE. If it is for one month or five years, we are going to do our best to find joy in every day!"

Defeat had filled my husband as I sat there holding him. Whispers came, "I love you, Jack."

I could barely muster up my voice to reply, "I love you too, sweets."

Then out of the silence he said, "I love the girls so much. I don't want to hurt them."

I immediately began praying for my husband to be at peace, to keep the fight, and have a willingness to live.

God is good, even when we might be in a huge storm! God is good!

I confidently stand in the belief of a miracle happening. My vision has always been complete healing of Doug. Miracles do happen! Even knowing the severity of the type of tumor we are up against, MIRACLES DO HAPPEN!

With the devastating news of tumor growth and rapid spreading, I am still choosing to hold onto hope, knowing God is in control and He can work miraculous healing. I will not give in to this without a fight. My faith is strong and my love for Doug is even stronger. I am a warrior standing firm for my husband and my girls.

2 Corinthians 4:8-9

We are hard pressed on every side, but not crushed; perplexed, but not in despair; persecuted, but not abandoned; struck down, but not destroyed.

When I called Z to let her know the results of the MRI, I, as a mom, was not prepared for what I would hear on the other end of the phone. The extreme crying, followed with, "Mom, why? Mom, why us?" Then more crying.

I wanted to get through that phone and hold my girl. It crushed me that I couldn't be there with her. It was her response that jolted me.

"Mom, I prayed. I prayed all day while I was in class. Why, why would God do this? I don't understand."

If I am completely honest, I also don't understand.

When we started this journey eighteen months ago, we had no idea what we would experience. The Lord knew what the plan was, but He didn't let us in on it. In eighteen months, my faith has blossomed, and I have taken a stand to share it with the world. We, as a family of five, saw our bond become stronger than we ever could have imagined. Christ was pulled back to the front of Doug's life, and my girls opened their hearts up to Him. Through our story, people's lives have been inspired and touched, and lessons continue to be taught and learned. Our story has reached thousands through various outlets. Complete strangers have sent messages of how we have inspired them or just messages of thanks. In our journey, we have met the most amazing doctors, nurses, front desk staff, and patients.

We continue to feel like we have always had a choice; we can get knocked down and stay down or we can get knocked down, stand up and ask, "Is that all?" We have a choice to drop our heads and mope or hold our heads high and share a smile. We have the choice to find the joy in every day—yes, even the really bad days.

While it might be normal to question what is happening to us, we don't get stuck on the question. We must trust in the Lord with the plan He has for us, believing that no matter where we go, He is by our side. Even in the moments we feel we are alone, He is near. Prayers are answered, but often not on our time schedule, and sometimes not in the way we would prefer.

Here is how I answer my girls: *Why us?* Because we have been chosen to share our strength and to allow complete strangers into our journey so they may be inspired or so they may vicariously feel our love. We are showing others that although it *is* tough, being vulnerable is actually very healthy. We are showing others it takes sticking together to fight and fight. Through our story, Christ has shone. *Why us?* Because the Lord knew from the beginning, we had it in us to survive and that we were willing and able to step up to the challenge!

Moments of weakness are normal, moments filled with frustration and tears will come, but moments of joy need to happen forever! With every storm, the sun still shines and rainbows emerge! We go through life wondering what tomorrow will bring and where we might be next week, which takes us into what may or may not ever happen. All the while we are doing that, we have missed the moment we are in.

There are no more medical trials for Doug to enter. We have decisions to make on chemo and what supplement regimen to use through the wellness clinic. But we have decided from now until the end WE WILL LIVE, and LIVE IN EVERY MOMENT! We will be loving on each other and finding joy! I am praying for a miracle! I will still pray for our miracle.

Isaiah 33:2

O Lord, be gracious to us; we long for you. Be our strength every morning, our salvation in time of distress.

Chapter Forty-three

How Strong Is Your Back?

CaringBridge Entry
September 11, 2015

Is my back strong enough to carry the weak? Is it strong enough to put my life on hold to care for a loved one? Is it strong enough to put on a smile, even when I could cry for days? Is it strong enough that when the bad days get worse, I can still stand upright? Is my back strong enough to be vulnerable? Is it strong enough to allow me to drop to my knees and pray?

The strength of my back has come from my choice to fight through adversity, to be steadfast in my faith, to look every moment in the face, and, despite it all, find a bit of joy. When I struggle to find strength, I rely on Jesus.

I must admit, my strength has been tested these past few days. With the conversations between the five of us, along with witnessing the heartache of my girls, and the depleted demeanor of my best friend, I have been tested. This storm we are facing has shown me how strong I can be, how strong my three girls are, and at the same time, it has shown us how weak we are. In weakness we lean on each other and Jesus.

Life seems to continue. At times, I wish it would slow down or even come to a complete stop.

I think it is interesting how we take the tender moments for granted, traveling through life so unaware, or maybe it's because we've got the it-won't-happen-to-me mentality.

It's so important to be in the moment. Each moment. Every single one of them. Don't wait to tell your mom how wonderful she is. Don't wait until the next practice to tell your coach how they have impacted you. Don't wait for the next time your sibling does something great to tell them. Don't wait for another opportunity to express your love and appreciation to a loved one. Don't wait until maybe it is too late!

Z has been home this week enjoying time with her dad. Today, they went to the field, and he threw front tosses to her. It was a good day. As we sat at the field, he said, "I forgot how much I love being out here." The simple things, even walking out onto a field, mean so much.

With Doug's unsteadiness, I decided it was easier to shower with him. As I washed his legs, he began to giggle.

I said, "What's so funny?"

He smiled a great big smile at me and said, "I can actually walk, but I want you to shower with me." We both giggled and then he looked me in the eyes and said, "Thank you for taking care of me, I am so lucky."

I then told him, "I'm pretty sure I am the lucky one!"

We are truly finding ways to enjoy every second together.

Chapter Forty-four
State Championship Ring

CaringBridge Entry
September 18, 2015

As the days go by, we continue to embrace the joy we have in each day. Doug is doing really well, his weakness on the left side seems to get worse when he sits or lies for too long. I am doing my best to keep him moving.

On Wednesday, we went out to the softball field where Doug received his state champion ring! The football coach sent the JV and varsity football teams over to surround Doug as the athletic director presented him with his ring. He openly cried and was so honored to put it on his finger.

As I watched him, I realized how much he has impacted young athletes. He is a true coach who always looks out for the best for his young players.

Looking back, I am in awe of watching girls grow up in the softball world. Doug would be coaching, and he would say, "Jack, this one has something special. You watch her grow; she is going to do amazing things!"

It has been fun, over the past twelve years of his coaching, watching those he talked about when they were little and growing up to do exactly what he said. They have done amazing things!

Doug has received sweet letters in the mail and all the loving posts on social media expressing how he has inspired, impacted, and believed in players. It has warmed my heart to see such beautiful writings about him.

It is as heartwarming to hear him say, "Oh my gosh! They are the reason I coach; they do all the work, Jack. I am there to guide them, to show them what I see in them."

He is the exact coach I would have handpicked for my three girls. He inspires, builds up his players, makes an impact, and believes and shows what being a part of a team truly means. Winning is fun. Winning makes for a good time, but coaching isn't about the scores between two teams.

Taking an athlete who doesn't believe in herself and helping her to see what he could see, putting his arm around an athlete when they've had a bad day, watching them achieve goals that might be so simple to the outside world, having an athlete he coached tell him years later how much he impacted them, that is what coaching is about. That is WINNING!

Doug truly exemplifies inspiration to his team and the whole softball world here in Idaho. His unwavering strength, the courage he displays for all to witness, and the love he has for his team completes the passion he has always had for coaching and building strong female athletes.

Chapter Forty-five

Great Weekend

It was a weekend full of alumni softball games. We drove four hours to Ogden for Weber State's alumni game.

They honored Doug in the fight against brain cancer. He threw out the first pitch with Z holding onto him. It was emotional and humbling to see these young girls and amazing coaches rally around and support my girl. Those coaches knew the true meaning of being a coach!

After a quick trip home from Utah, we went from church straight to the College of Idaho to watch Bentli play in her alumni game. It was a busy weekend full of so much joy!

Doug loved watching his girls play. I'm so proud of their hard work and determination to do great things! Although we were having more not-so-good days, we were trying to savor every moment we could. It was good for the girls to see their dad in the stands watching as well.

Due to his left-side weakness, he depended on help walking and standing. Therefore, I was his constant, giving him the help he needed and making sure whoever took my place had a tight hold on him.

He was completely exhausted from the busy weekend but would not change a thing.

For the most part I held strong for him, but watching the movements get weaker and weaker I had more flashes of disbelief at what we were facing, causing more tears to be shed.

Psalms 77:13-14

Your ways, O God, are holy. What god is so great as our God? You are the God who performs miracles; you display your power among the peoples.

Every morning, as I walked in to help Doug out of bed, I said to him. "Guess what?"

He replied, "The sun is up!"

I kissed him and said, "Yes, it is!" I was so grateful to share the beauty of the day.

With his left-side weakness, he had no movement in his left arm and hand. He walked with a crutch under his right arm and some "arm candy" on his left side! Most of the time it was me, or his good friends, or his daughters. Either way, he had to have assistance with his walking.

I was in charge of dressing him and putting his shoes on. With every little thing I did for him, it was his tender "thank you" that melted my heart.

I told him, "Sweets, you do not have to thank me for this, I love taking care of you."

He looked me in the eyes and said, "Thank you, thank you for loving me!"

CaringBridge Entry
September 25, 2015

Honestly, being a caregiver is a lot of work; it is time consuming and exhausting. But when your loved one is in need, there is not even a question. We do whatever possible to help them.

The Lord sure has an amazing plan for us. In times of questioning, we are reminded of greatness that is happening around us. We may not know the plan, but we are learning that the plan is bigger than we can imagine. Blessed! We are truly blessed!

The girls are all trying to deal with, figure out, and learn what this process is and what this journey consists of.

We sat on the bed before Z left to go back to school. She said, "Mom, I pray for a miracle, but I am also at peace if Jesus needs Dad in heaven more than we need him. Jesus knows we will be okay and will take care of us. Not that I'm giving up on a miracle, but I know God has a plan for us and we will be okay."

Shock hit me as she spoke these words.

Honestly, I internally questioned where I was with this. My conclusion was, *nope I am not at peace if Jesus needed her dad more*. Selfishly, I needed him here. They needed their dad here.

Wisdom like I had not experienced radiated from her words.

Bentli remarked that she was happy her sister had some peace, but she was plain mad!

Demi was quiet.

That is the realness of what is going on. I am proud of all three of them, being where they are in this process. Being mad is real! Being quiet is real! Being wise is real! We will be okay. We will survive because we are a family with a bond no one will ever be able to break.

Doug is scheduled for another MRI in Seattle in October; he is debating if he is going to have it done. He is only using supplements from the wellness clinic and takes a steroid to keep the headaches down. No chemo. Lots of prayers and hope!

Doug and I giggle a lot. The girls giggle a lot with us too. We share a smile with all who come into contact with us. I have always told my girls that one simple smile might make someone's day. It really is the easiest gift to give!

We are always given opportunities in our journey to reach out, share our stories, and show others compassion and caring. It is our choice to act on those things. I will definitely be working on my compassion for those who might benefit from it.

1 Peter 3:8

Finally, all of you, live in harmony with one another; be sympathetic, love as brothers, be compassionate and humble.

Chapter Forty-six

Today I Cried

I'm beginning to question if it would be easier to lose a loved one in an accident rather than deal with an illness. It's quick, it's done immediately, and there is no time to think. With an illness, you do get time to prepare, you do get time to say your goodbyes, you do get to love on them knowing time is short. But at the same time, you see your loved one who was once so strong become weak, you get to feel the sadness as they struggle, you find yourself consumed by so many things. Every little thing they face, your mind goes straight to, *Could this be the end?*

Although you still have your loved one with you, you begin to miss them. I missed dancing in my kitchen and being goofy with Doug. He was the one who drove me everywhere; but I had to drive him everywhere. I missed having both his arms around me, holding me, and knowing he would always keep me safe. I had to learn to hold him, comfort him, and tell him I loved taking care of him. I missed the strength he gave us as a husband and father.

I'm the one who kept my family together, and all the while I wanted to fall apart. Life didn't slow because my husband had cancer. I battled with myself, kept businesses going to support my family, and spent time with my husband. The bills didn't stop coming. Family needs were always there—girls needed this, girls needed that, and things fell apart at the restaurant that needed to be dealt with.

The stress of my sick husband, plus the stress of wondering how my three babies were truly doing, and all the daily tasks of life made my insides feel like they were going to explode some days. But I knew it was me to keep this family in check, so I found something to soothe that explosive feeling.

While there was a lot of stress, there was also the frustration that came to me. Getting ready for the day was not just me putting myself together. I had to put Douglas together too and with very little help because of the weakness in his left side.

I often got started doing something and I was called to help get him to the bathroom. I got pills ready. I gave him pills. I prepared breakfast, lunch, and dinner for him. As soon as I sat down to relax, I was called to get more water, or take him to bed, or take him back to the bathroom. I was frustrated that it was always me doing everything.

We had an agreement at the start of this marriage of fifty-fifty, so we did everything fifty-fifty. Where did that go?

I was frustrated. It was me awakened in the middle of the night to help him use the bathroom or to help him roll over because the weakness kept him from doing it by himself. I was frustrated beyond words that cancer was slowly taking my husband from me.

None, and I mean none, of those frustrations were toward my sweet husband! All these frustrations were completely toward cancer!

When I was thinking the day would be a good one, a day where I felt like I had it all together, I was plowed over by something. I was the one who got the text or phone calls from my girls. "Mom, I'm going to class with swollen eyes because I cried all night." I was the one who heard the sheer heartache when they said, "Mom, I'm scared!" It was always me who listened as tears streamed down their faces as they tried to get the words out about their hurt. It was me who held them as they talked about seeing posts of friends having dad's weekend with their dads, and it was the pure fact that they knew Douglas couldn't drive to see them. It was me who had to pull it together to keep us all going.

I was never aware how damaging cancer could be. It could actually tear a family and home apart. I chose to not allow that to happen to my family and home. I stayed rock solid. I was steadfast in my faith. I was a support to many. I was an inspiration and warrior. And I had many to support me.

CaringBridge Entry
October 9, 2015

Yet today, I have cried!

Although I have been so strong, the realness is that the love of my life is facing death. My heart aches, my mind wanders, and I struggle to grasp what my girls are going through. My love for Douglas has grown beyond what I thought it ever could be. At this moment I want to scream and cry and throw a fit about what cancer is doing in our lives, but I am also reminded of the good it is also doing—it is bringing in so much good!

The love between two people has blossomed into a beautiful love story. Strength has been shown to a family that was already pretty strong. Faith was restored and brought to the front line.

So, with all the stresses, with all my frustrations, with all the me-time that is pushed aside, I would walk this journey over and over and over again right by your side, Douglas. Holding the bowl while you puke, rubbing your head when the pain is so bad, wiping your tears as we cry together, dressing your cute butt when you cannot do it yourself, holding you in MY arms, feeling YOU protect me, learning what a warrior looks like, a champion, a true champion! So, if we could go back in time, I would grab your hand, stand firm in my stance, and I would say to cancer, "BRING IT ON, you do not scare me!"

My heart is full of so much love for my little family of five. We are not sure how long the rest of this journey will be, but we will make it the best of times! We hold onto a miraculous victory from God but trust in His plan for us!

A dear friend sent this to me:

"As we make Christ the center of our lives, our fears will be replaced by the courage of our convictions."

THIS SUCKS! That is the realness of this journey right now.

I have been humbled and overwhelmed; I have been filled with love, and I have been shedding tears.

I am humbled by the overflowing love of people my sweet husband has touched. Humbled knowing as he walked his path on this journey, he reached many, teaching lessons, planting seeds, and being the champion he has always been. I continue to be humbled tremendously by knowing how many young lives he has reached and has inspired, motivated, and believed in!

I am overwhelmed with the whole journey!

I am filled with love as my house is constantly full of family and friends! Loved with meals, groceries, cookies, and food to put in my freezer. Filled with love that for the last two nights, my living room floor has been covered with those who love Doug! We had a giant slumber party, with Doug sleeping in his chair! Filled with love knowing, as difficult as this is right now, the Lord has a much bigger plan than the plan Doug and I have. We were supposed to grow old together, travel watching our three girls play out their collegiate careers, spoil our grandbabies, and sit back and watch what amazing things our girls accomplish.

I have shed tears! I have shed numerous tears of complete sadness for my girls, watching what is happening to their daddy! Tears for myself because my best friend is in this situation! I have shed tears as I pray for whatever it is the Lord needs. I have shed the tears of knowing he might be needed in heaven more than I need him here.

My heart hurts, I have had this amazing man in my life since I was fifteen years old. Thinking of life without his physical body next to me makes me sick to my stomach and my heart break.

As we keep up this fight, until the last breath, I am also realistic on the severity of this vicious tumor. We continue to pray for a miraculous victory that we can rejoice in. We trust in our Heavenly Father. Although we think we know what's best, we need to trust! So, I continue to stand firm in my faith, believing that where our journey goes is exactly where we are meant to be!

I am so honored to have this gracious man by my side, the love of my life that has taught me so much about life. He has shown me how to touch lives and how to be true to who you are, never allowing others to influence you into something you are not.

He has shown me what hard work looks like, and how it pays off. He has taught his three girls to never expect anything to be given; he has taught them that through their work ethic, passion, and commitment is the only way to achieve goals in life.

Spouses, love your spouses, love them every day! Even those days they piss you off. Find the love you share and love them.

Young people, love your daddy! Don't take for granted the love they have for you. Those moments when you feel he doesn't understand you, doesn't seem to care what you want, doesn't feel as if he loves you, love him anyway! For it is in those moments his heart is so full of love for you! Take the time to show your appreciation for every little thing he does. In a blink of an eye, he could be gone!

TEAM CORTA: We are so loved!

Jeremiah 29:11

> *"For I know the plans I have for you," declares the Lord, "plans to prosper you and not to harm you, plans to give you hope and a future."*

WHEN YOUR MIRACLE *Doesn't Come*

Chapter Forty-seven

190 Notes

I was completely taken aback. In the mail, we received a package from Weber State University Athletics. Inside we found handwritten notes. All from WSU athletes from football, softball, women's and men's basketball, women's and men's tennis, track and field, women's and men's golf, women's soccer, and volleyball. Not a note of "thinking of you" or "sending prayers." They were heartfelt, encouraging, and completely full of love.

One hundred ninety notes from young athletes, coaches, and administration. As I read each note, I was overwhelmed and humbled by the outpouring of love and support for our family and my girl Z!

I questioned how a university of this size would pull together for one athlete and her family. I found out the athlete who put this together wasn't even in the softball program. It warmed my heart.

In today's world, we hear of the athletes getting kicked off teams, drugs being done, suspensions for all sorts of things, and probations put in place. It is this story I would hope could travel the nation. One hundred ninety athletes being selfless, showing a tender side, supporting one of their own, being not only an athlete but being a family!

I am so honored to be part of the Weber State family! I am completely blessed my girl Z is at such an amazing university. The words THANK YOU do not do justice! My heart is full of so much love and encouragement. *Weber State Athletics, you are doing life right!* I would hope all 190 would see and feel my gratitude!

Chapter Forty-eight

Wow

I woke up to an amazing, special tribute to my husband on my lawn.

When I walked out of the house to go to church, I was shocked at what I saw. There were ninety-one bright yellow softballs, perfectly placed in a six-foot-wide heart. The front ball in bold black marker said TEAM CORTA.

I turned to get Doug to see this magnificent tribute. As I walked closer, I saw that every single ball had a message on it. There were ninety-one softballs with heartfelt messages to a coach from his girls. Most were from girls he had coached, and others were players he had coached against. Each ball was from a special girl that Doug had touched. The messages on each ball were so moving.

Coaches, ask yourselves are you coaching young athletes with love and the willingness to build character over getting a W?

This showed me Doug was coaching for ALL the right reasons! I was honored!

Reading every message, and understanding how my husband touched these young lives, was humbling.

"Coach, thanks for believing in me when no one else did."

"It is you who pushed me to be the best athlete I could be, and I am so grateful for that."

"Your dance moves at practice will always bring a smile to my face."

"Coach, you are simply the best coach I have ever had."

Doug was taken aback by what he saw; he sat there in his wheelchair staring down at all the balls.

Z grabbed one and read it out loud, as he just shook his head. I held his hand and told him, "Do you see the impact you have had on these girls? Some you have never coached!"

He said, "I can't believe this; what sweet girls."

The outpouring of love with this kind gesture had him overwhelmed with emotions. As Z kept reading, tears began to fall.

She said, "Dad I can stop reading them out loud. I don't want to upset you."

Wiping his eyes, he replied, "No, I want to hear all of them; it is just a lot to take in."

We moved him and all the softballs into the house where each ball was read. He held many in his hands or lap for quite some time.

———————

CaringBridge Entry
October 16, 2015

Doug has had good days and he has had bad days. We spend most of our days resting or watching some TV. Visitors come and go and in each, we find comfort. The hospice nurse comes three times a week, checks his vitals, and visits with us. His vitals have all read strong. Blood pressure good. Heart at a strong beat. No temperature.

On good mornings when Doug has more strength and is not as listless, we enjoy breakfast on the deck. Cool air, comfy blankets, hot coffee, running water in the creek, and good company doesn't get any better!

Z returned to Weber on Sunday; it was a hard "see you soon."

Bent went to classes, but stayed at home, and I got Demi back to school as well.

Tonight, we all went to the Eagle High football game. We loaded Doug up in his wheelchair, with his blankets and his state championship letterman jacket. We wheeled him down to the corner of the end zone where we always stand to watch the game. There were handshakes to many and lots of *good to see you*s and *love you*s were spoken.

The fresh air was so nice, although it cooled off quickly. Doug was ready to get home and back to his recliner, so we decided to leave a few minutes into the third quarter.

As we were headed out to the car, two young boys walked up and stopped us. "Excuse me, can I shake your hand?" they asked.

Doug reached his hand out and the first boy said, "Thank you!"

The second boy stepped in and reached his hand toward Doug. As he shook Doug's hand, he also said, "Thank you. Thank you so much." Then off they trotted back toward the stadium.

I stood there in disbelief. Z mouthed to me, "Who are they?"

I shrugged my shoulders because I didn't know them. I told Z I would catch up to her at the car, and I quickly walked back to the stadium and caught up with the athletic director before the boys got out of sight. I told her what took place and asked her to talk to the boys. I wanted to know how they knew Doug and what they were thanking him for.

When we went home and I got Doug in his recliner to rest, I got a call from the athletic director. She told me she talked to the boys. She asked them if they saw Doug Corta tonight, and they quickly said, "Yep, we even shook his hand."

She asked them how they knew him.

One responded, "We know his daughter Demi, and I read his Facebook posts and know his story."

The other said, "Yeah, and I play for the JV football team and was there when you gave him his state championship ring; that was so cool." They explained that they wanted to say thanks for coming out and supporting them at the game.

I was completely shocked, and a lump came into my throat. This is what cancer is doing for us. *Why would I ever think cancer is so bad when I can see all the good that comes with it?* I would love to meet those boys again, and this time, I would ask to shake *their* hands! I love that there are innocent lives being touched and young people being moved to leave the game to come over to us for a simple handshake.

In this journey we all call life, it is truly about love! It's about showing love in every relationship we encounter. No matter how big or small, it is about showing love; the love that is shown with a genuine smile, kind words of encouragement, or a simple handshake!

One thing we are all lucky to have is the ability to choose. But for some reason, most choose to see the bad in things instead of the good.

Who cares about the hand you're dealt? Choose to make the best of it! Choose to be happy. Even on your worst day, find something in it that makes you happy. Choose to love and be sure to love wholeheartedly. Choose to make a difference because we all have the chance to make a difference at some point. Choose to see the good that can come from something bad (like cancer) in your life.

Doug and I chose at the beginning of this journey that we were not going to allow cancer to run our lives. We chose to live the best life we could and chose to share our journey, hoping we would touch one soul. We learned we have touched more than one.

In the darkness cancer can bring, small acts are like rays of hope that stand in the shadows.

I rejoiced every morning I had with Doug. I was thankful Christ had been shining through Doug and our family. I was at peace with the plan that had been put in place!

What does that mean? I surrendered to the Lord and what He needed from me, and the life Doug was living, even if that life was calling him home.

This did not minimize what we faced or the fight we were fighting. Instead, it provided a calm inside of me. Peace brought a new understanding to what my journey was, and it gave light to the heaviness that was imminent. Hope and believing in a miracle were still present in the fight, but I felt the Lord giving me some realistic thoughts.

The days seemed to come and go. We enjoyed every single second we had. We kept Doug's pain level down and he still had an appetite.

We had all the girls home one week. I was grateful to the professors and coaches that were so understanding. And I am beyond proud of my girls who kept pushing forward in their schoolwork in that difficult time.

When you are thrown into a journey that is challenging, I believe you have a choice. But in making choices to be strong, to fight, to stand firm in your faith, to love every situation, to embrace the hard times, and to celebrate each small victory, there are moments of weakness, sadness, anger, and disbelief.

It happened when Bentli ran out the door with tears flowing down her face, Z racing after to make sure she was okay. I realized I couldn't run out with them and share in their grief. I had to pull it together to try to find some comfort for them.

I walked out the door and started searching for them in the dark. They were sitting up the street on the sidewalk. Bent was crying while Z was holding her. I walked up and sat down on the sidewalk in my jammies next to them.

I immediately said, "I'm sorry, I should have warned you."

The reason she was sobbing was because we were changing Doug's shirt and she saw his frail body for the first time.

"It feels like a horrible nightmare, Mom, and I want to wake up. I want it to go away." Z began to cry alongside her. I wrapped my arm around Bent, as she continued, "Why can't it go away?"

I whispered to the both of them, "If I could take it away, I would. I would take it all away."

Z said, "I know there must be a plan, but I don't understand."

Bent followed up with, "Others survive, why can't Dad?"

We sat there in the dark crying. Out of the silence Z said, "Mom, do you think we are all going to get cancer?"

I quickly replied, "No, I do not think we all will get cancer. Although we can't see the plan right now, God has to have something big for us."

The grief process can start before we even lose a loved one, especially with a prolonged illness. Observing our loved one as he slowly declined in health and strength created lots of feelings. We may not have even known or understood we were grieving.

I watched my very strong husband come to have a weak body. He could only stand with my help. Food got in his body only when I fed him small bites. I am the one who held his frail body on the toilet so he wouldn't slip off. When he got so sick and couldn't stop vomiting, I sat there holding the bowl, wiping his mouth, comforting him. Dressing him was my job as well.

Through all of this, every time, he whispered, "Thank you!"

I always responded, "You are so welcome, but please don't thank me. I love taking care of you."

In his weakness, in the moments of complete sickness, he was not drawn into his distress; rather, he was only thinking of me and showing me his complete, true love, his selflessness, his compassion. I was blessed with the best!

We faced adversity straight on and refused to let it define us. I sat in church one Sunday listening to a man speak of his rare disease, how sick he was, the prayers he received, and the huge miracle he got. Complete healing!

This was the real me: It took everything for me to stay seated in the pew. I wanted to walk out; I did not want to listen to his miracle. Don't get me wrong, I love that he was blessed with complete healing, but it stirred up my emotions.

I hold my faith to a high standard, but I DON'T UNDERSTAND! I don't understand why Doug was going through this, why my girls had to live this, or why we endured so much pain. I know it is part of life to not always understand. Being strong in our faith doesn't mean we don't have moments of not understanding. We had so many praying for us, we stood steadfast in our faith, and we were *not* getting our miracle.

I continued to watch the love of my life decline in health as he so diligently fought for his life. My mom heart ached thinking about the three young girls who loved their dad more than anything.

I threw up my arms, expressing to the Lord I DO NOT UNDERSTAND! I kept praying for complete healing over Doug's body, for comfort for my three girls, and strength for myself.

Numerous people have expressed, "You are the strongest person I know."

"Your strength is unbelievable."

"You shine Christ's love through your smile."

Let me say that as strong as I was, I wept an enormous number of tears. My battle continued, our game plan changed, we played a new defense, but never did I sub out my number one player who is the Lord above!

I found myself weepier, confused, and not understanding. When I noticed more husbands with their wives, I'd also notice a lump in my throat. When I saw daddies with their babies, I wanted to run up to them and tell them to cherish each second; I turned away and let tears well in my eyes. My journey was ongoing, and although I had moments of weakness, my heart was full of love, my soul was filled with memories, and my life had been blessed by many.

I held on to that.

Chapter Forty-nine

My Heart Is Broken

CaringBridge Entry
November 6, 2015

My heart is completely broken. The love of my life, my best friend, and the best dad to my three amazing girls was welcomed home in Heaven.

Our hearts are hurting, our tears won't stop, we are holding each other and feeling numb at the same time. I have lost half of myself. The words that usually flow right out of me seem to be at a halt. I'm guessing that is because I have always written from my heart, and it is broken right now. This journey has been one heck of a ride, and I can honestly say we took it with our heads held high, our faith in the front, and we fought until the end.

You will never hear me say "He lost his battle to cancer." THAT IS A LIE!

When cancer entered our lives, we first saw it as a battle and approached it in that way when we needed to, but then over time, we realized it *wasn't* a battle, it was a process instead. The Lord knew this was what we needed to be able to reach thousands of souls. Through this process, we have learned, we have taught, we have inspired, we have questioned, we have planted seeds, we have shown the beauty cancer can bring, and we have had Christ right next to us to share with everyone.

2 Timothy 4:7

I have fought the good fight, I have finished the race, I have kept the faith.

My love walks in the heavens with no pain, with no weakness.

My Dearest Doug,

You can coach Heaven's team now.

The Lord needed you more, and now with your angel wings, you can touch more young athletes than ever before.

No battles lost, my love, your job here was finished. Although we shed tears and might not fully understand, I know you lived a Christ-filled life. And the work you did for Him is shining through numerous souls today!

Thank you for loving me and being my best friend. The girls and I will forever carry on your name and promise to coach, love, and mentor others as you did!

I love your guts! Promise!

Until we walk eternity together!

My phone began filling up with texts from family and friends sending me pictures of the most beautiful sunrise with messages of "look what Doug sent you this morning." "Look at the beauty in this sunrise; praying for you."

My house filled up with family and friends as I sat in the living room where Doug passed, completely numb. I can't recall a lot of that day, but I do know the girls distanced themselves from the crowd forming in our home.

There was a point where the four of us ended up in Bentli's room sitting on her bed.

I made my way back upstairs; I think I felt like I needed to be seen by all who were entering my house. The girls, on the other hand, wanted to stay isolated. The shock was so apparent and the comfort from others was not wanted.

Having my mom present was so helpful. She made sure food was getting fixed for us all and kept my house in order.

I felt blessed by all the love I received.

There are three things that bring my soul peace. Being at my grandparents' ranch, on the basketball court, and writing. Since I can't get to the ranch yet, and there is no basketball court for me to be on, I decided I would write.

My tears don't seem to stop. I had no idea the pain one could feel from a broken heart. I am finding out… I was not prepared. We always knew the devastation this tumor could cause, but I will be honest, I truly thought we would get our miracle. I did not believe it would take Doug. My heart aches for him, my ears miss his voice, my arms miss wrapping around his body, and my soul is as sad as it could possibly be.

I'm trying to get through each day knowing I will be alone, and my oh-so-young girls will continue life without a daddy! There will be a new normal, one that might take some time to get used to.

The four of us have had talks of what I expect and what Dad would want for us. We will continue to do life with all the expectations Doug had for the girls. We will grieve, then we will find the new normal intertwined with those expectations. The bond the five of us have is not broken because one went home to Jesus. If anything, it will strengthen our connection and bind us more closely.

Knowing Doug is near, and I can talk and know he hears me, brings me some peace.

Friday morning after he passed, I walked out to the garbage. I looked to the beautiful sky and started to cry. Out loud I spoke, "I miss you already, and I need to know you are still by my side. Right here by me still."

I walked in the house and sat in the chair by the bar. My sister was sitting in the far barstool; there were two stools closer to me. The stools squeak when you sit down on them. As I sat in the chair, one stool next to me started to squeak. I turned to look, and my sister gave me a look that said she was wondering why it was squeaking all by itself.

I began to bawl, and I said, "Thank You! Thank you for allowing me to know you are near!" That barstool squeaked for two minutes.

I am grateful for the twenty-two years I got to walk this earth with him by my side, and I know one day I will spend eternity with him in heaven. The Lord blessed our family with two amazing years with Doug, fighting through adversity, making choices to be the best, and always being as true and real as we could be. I appreciated seeing what life was about, how small things really are, and loving each other like we had never loved before.

Celebrating Doug's life is going to be the most amazing and the most heart-wrenching thing I will ever do. I am trusting in the Lord to not only help us through this moment in our life, but I am trusting in His plan. Although I may not understand right now, and it might hurt, and the tears have not dried at all, I believe He has something so grand for the four of us. I also believe Douglas will be right here with us.

TEAM CORTA STRONG!

Deuteronomy 31:6

Be strong and courageous. Do not be afraid or terrified because of them, for the Lord your God goes with you; he will never leave you nor forsake you.

Chapter Fifty

Doug's Celebration of Life

As I stood in the back of the church that Saturday waiting to walk down the aisle, I quickly thought, *Where is my dad?* The last time a church was this full and I was walking down the aisle, my dad was holding my arm. It was my wedding day; Douglas was standing at the front with the biggest smile as I walked toward him. This time, I was walking alone with my girls following, Douglas was at the front, and I am sure he was smiling just as big, but from heaven.

I walked as slowly as I did on our wedding day, feeling so many eyes on me. This time, they weren't admiring my gorgeous wedding gown, or how my hair was done, but yearning to see how I was holding up, how my girls were doing.

The amount of love I could feel coming from each person, pierced my soul. The small bit of anxiousness was calmed. As we approached the front where we would sit, I continued to follow the usher to the stairs. The girls sat down as I placed myself at the podium. *Deep breath*, I told myself, *stay strong, you can do this.* And I began to speak:

> *I knew that to truly honor Douglas, I had to speak. I pondered what I would say. I could stand up here all day and tell you what an amazing husband he was to me. I could*

tell you he was the best dad for my three girls. I have so many amazing stories I could share about his coaching years.

But as I sat down to write, I decided I had so much more I wanted to share. I had things Doug and I had talked about; things he'd want me to share.

Twenty months ago, we were faced with the biggest challenge ever. Cancer entered our lives. I remember one of the girls saying, "He is going to die. Mom, cancer means death." But I quickly reminded her there are many who outlive a cancer diagnosis. Doug and I had decided, we were not going to be defined by the word cancer. We were not going to let it scare us. Together we were going to fight and when we got knocked down, we agreed we were going to stand up and continue the fight.

You see, we quickly learned about the beauty that cancer brings to people's life. Once you face what we had been facing, your outlook on life changes. You speak a bit softer, you anger less, you cherish more, and you love on a much deeper level. I can truly say cancer made me fall in love all over and I loved at a deeper level than I ever could have imagined.

Adversity stood as a roadblock in this journey we were on. Instead of becoming weak or weeping in our sorrows, we knew we had choices. So the five of us chose to stand together, to stand firm in our faith, and to trust in what was to be. We chose to live. We chose to enjoy every day. And we chose to share a smile.

For all the couples here today, my message is to love each other. Even when they are driving you crazy, stop and remember why you fell in love with them in the first place.

Hold their hand more, giggle more, snuggle more, and write, or rewrite, your own love story.

To all the coaches here today, I encourage you to reevaluate how you are coaching; start by asking yourself why you are coaching. Is it for the title? Is it for the glory of victory? Or are you coaching to mentor young athletes in the game of life? Are you building character before a "W"? Step back and ask yourself, would you have ninety softballs left on your lawn, each with a message of hope, of gratitude, of respect? I always knew Doug coached for the girls!

Athletes that are scattered through this sanctuary, listen to what I have to say. You will face adversity; it will come to you through all kinds of things—some bigger than others. The beauty of adversity is that you have a choice with what you want to do with it, how you will respond. I ask you when your adversity hits, remember Coach Corta. Reflect on how he looked adversity in the face and chose to keep going and to push through when it felt like he had no energy. He— we—chose to fight and to keep fighting!

To my three girls, I love your guts, we will be okay. It will take some time to heal. You girls have way too much of dad in you to have a different outcome; he made you as strong as you are. His strength will now strengthen you. The bond the five of us have is not broken because one of us went home to Jesus. It only has been made stronger! Love you to the moon and back forever and always!

Thank you for being here, and for walking alongside us. It mattered. You mattered. You helped us more than you can realize.

Love and Blessings to All!

Then, I slowly walked to my seat and sat with my girls. The videos we played were put together beautifully. All were gut-wrenching and fervent, and they completely showcased Douglas exquisitely.

Our pastor honored Doug as he should be honored. He spoke gracefully and from the heart. The family and friends that we chose to speak warmed my heart with every word they spoke. I felt so proud to be his wife. Many tears were shed, and I pulled myself together to follow the casket out of the church.

My tears began as soon as the pallbearers walked to the front. There stood the men Doug had chosen to help lay him to rest. I could recall our conversation on why he chose each one, what they meant to him, things they had enjoyed together. I was overcome with sadness and tears.

I grabbed Bentli's hand, and we followed the casket with Z and Demi right behind.

It could not have been a better November day; the sun was shining, and it was close to sixty degrees.

The time at the graveside was quick. I sat there staring at the casket, listening, once again, to our pastor speaking from his heart, knowing my final goodbye was coming. I had told the girls that once the pastor was done, I was not going to stay.

This part I knew I wasn't so good with—something about being in a box, in the ground, outside, and cold. I just know I don't handle it so well. So, as it was coming to a close, my emotions built, and my tears streamed. Once he finished, I stood up next to the casket and said, "I love your guts… PROMISE!" And bolted. In fact, if I hadn't been in those heels I would have sprinted to the car.

It was nice to see everyone at the dinner. I love hugs, but wow, I had no idea I would receive that many. I truly felt the love and support. It brought me great comfort to see the spectacular support the girls and I were getting.

Doug would have been shaking his head that close to fifteen hundred people filled the church to honor him. He would have loved the stories being told about him and all his adventures through life. It was such a humbling day. I could not have asked for it to go any better, and I stood proud as Doug Corta's wife.

Then came the silence.

Chapter Fifty-one

What Happens Next?

With family gone home and friends no longer there, the silence set in. My house had been chaos for the last week, and then, suddenly, it was just the four of us.

Sunday, I went and sat at Doug's graveside. I took a coffee and a blanket. I sat with the wind blowing and feeling a sense of peace. It's funny how I felt complete peace just before the tears began to run down my face.

I felt selfish. I yearned for his presence, knowing it would take the heartache away if he was there. I was making it about myself and not the big picture, which is okay in those times. All I wanted was him there with me.

We preached to our girls that selfishness will get you nothing. Life is about being selfless. And there I was being so selfish. I allowed myself to cry. For thirty minutes, I sat and cried. I cried and then I wrote.

CaringBridge Entry
November 20, 2015

There is not a day that I don't cry my eyes out. If I could pool my tears and sit in a raft, they would have already raised me into the clouds where I could dance with Doug in heaven one last time. I have never felt heartache the way I feel right now. I have never missed someone the way I miss him. I had no idea sadness could consume a person's whole being!

Sleep is overrated. Or maybe it is scary. I sleep—well technically, I sit until my eyes close, in the chair in the living room with lights on and the TV going. Most of the time, 2:30 or 3:00 a.m. is the last time I look at the clock. Then, I'm up around 4:30 or 5:00 a.m. My mind seems to never shut off, but my energy level is diminished.

I hope one day soon I will find the desire to do something outside of my home. I guess it is comforting to be here. Plus, my eyes leak at times I am not prepared for, so it is easier to be here and have them leak than out and about.

I read every text, comment, and message I get. I love reading them and they bring me comfort. There are so many, and I can't seem to respond to them all.

I can honestly say my faith has weakened trying to understand why the Lord would want this pain for anyone. Don't get me wrong, I know I am not the only one who has faced this. But this is my true self talking.

Do I trust in His plan? Yes. Trust He knows what we need? Yes. Trust He will be next to us giving us strength? Yes. But I also want to scream from the top of my lungs that I and my girls are enduring unimaginable pain.

Do I believe, in time, my faith will be strengthened? Yes. And do I believe my hurt will become less? Yes! In time, joy will enter my life again? Yes! But until that time comes, I will continue to be.

I wrote twenty months ago about our lives being turned upside down and how the Lord reached down and pulled us to our feet. I truly thought that was the hardest moment in this journey. But when you stand together, fighting like we were, believing and trusting, and the end result is not the one you were planning for, your world is turned upside down again.

But this time I am struggling to grasp hold of Christ's hand to pull me to my feet. Not because I don't trust, or I have lost my faith, but because, right now, as I sit in the pit of sadness, dwelling on my broken heart, it is Christ being patient with me, allowing me to take the time I need before I reach for His hand.

Shock is such a huge part of grief and here I am in the trenches, not knowing if I will ever get out. I am giving myself grace to feel and be exactly where I am and not allowing anyone to take me from it.

———————

Your grief journey is yours and no one else's. You also get to travel it how you need to. If life strikes you with a scenario where you will be facing grief, I encourage you to give yourself grace as you go through it.

Psalm 119:28

My soul is weary with sorrow; strengthen me according to your word.

I recall the night in the ER when we were told there was what they would call a "lesion."

There was a shift in me. I knew in my heart Doug would be healed. I believed this diagnosis was not going to take my husband. There were weddings to walk brides down the aisle, there were grandbabies to spoil, love on, and send home to their parents. We had traveling to do. We wanted to watch our girls play softball. We had college graduations to attend and then quiet nights at home to look forward to with an empty house. We were to grow old, retire, and have time to do whatever we wanted. But what we wanted and what the Lord designs are two different things.

For twenty months, my mission was to fight. I was completely convinced we were going to get the miracle we needed. Even in the end when we were told to get hospice, I was standing firm in my faith; I was trusting in God's plan for us.

I did not see how sick Douglas was in that last month. I was in survival mode, warrior mode. It was after he passed, and I looked back at pictures, that I saw how sick he was.

I said to my cousin, "I did not see this version of Doug; I never saw him this sick."

It has taken a bit, but I now see and acknowledge that we, in fact, have witnessed what we all prayed for. From the beginning, I believed and prayed for a miracle. I prayed for complete healing over my husband. All the while, for twenty months, I saw MRI after MRI with new growth, new spots, and treatment after treatment that was not working. Do this chemo, wait, now do this chemo. More radiation, oh, and then some more radiation.

But through this journey, everything I had prayed for was happening right in front of me.

I prayed for complete healing.

Now, I realize that Doug *was* completely healed.

What does complete healing really mean?

For most of us, it means no more sickness, more years together, and living here on this earth. But now, I have come to believe that complete healing *had* happened within Doug. He was healed, but the problem was he was not *cured*!

Through the cancer, he was healed within himself. He found a compassion I had never seen in our twenty years of marriage, compassion that came solely from a Christ-filled heart. There was a relationship with Christ that returned to the front of his life.

Miracles *were* happening the whole time. There were miracles with Douglas getting stable MRIs along with strength in his body to be able to go back to the dugout for coaching. We were able to share our story, and miracles were taking place for many who were reading and sharing our story. Lives were being changed, hearts softened, seeds planted; there was a glow around us. Yes, Douglas had cancer, but cancer brought us more than we ever thought it could.

When people get the diagnosis of "cancer, I'm sorry but it is cancer" the majority of society stops right there. They don't ever get past the diagnosis. They know the horrors of cancer, they know the sickness of cancer, they only hear *cancer*, which in their minds says, *I am going to die!* So immediately the fight they think they have is weakened.

Cancer brought us relationships we would have never had. Incredible nurses and doctors came into our life. Other cancer patients were part of our team. It didn't matter what type of cancer they had; cancer is one team. By sharing our journey with cancer, we found relationships with people who had been distant. We had strangers send us words of encouragement, and we were encouraging many, as well.

When your life is over, there is one question asked: Did you do what you were supposed to do?

We can get caught up in living and trying to reach the highest position at our jobs or buying the biggest or best house and car, all the while pushing our family to the sideline as we run this race to achieve.

But in reality, we need to pause and listen to what the Lord has for us. We need to be running after Him. Maybe we are facing something *because* it will impact others.

My hope is that one soul can be reached and changed and that seeds can be planted, so a new life can begin with a joy that has never been felt. And I hope my story can begin a shift in that story.

We chose to not allow cancer to take our identity. We were going to give cancer a different identity. In the moment you hear these three words "It is cancer," your life is changed forever, but you have a choice as to what you will let cancer change or how you will let it change you.

I will never forget a conversation Douglas and I had. We were in our home, sitting in our living room, when he said to me, "Jack, can I tell you something?"

I figured this is where I was going to hear, "I love you" or "Thank you for being so good to me." But that was not what I heard that day. In his soft-spoken voice he said, "Jack, if my having cancer can help one person, or can give insight to the doctors for a cure, I am okay having it."

I began to cry, and replied, "You, my dear, are so selfless to be thinking of others while you are fighting your own fight."

He looked at me with tears in his eyes and said, "I think I was picked to fight this fight because we know a lot of people, Jack, so if we keep sharing our story, others can be inspired or maybe changed; maybe through my fight someone can win theirs."

I remember saying, "Well, we are going to win this fight of our own, and touch lives as we do it."

He graciously said, "But if it doesn't work out…" Tears flowing down his face as I grabbed his hand, he laid his head on my shoulder and whispered, "Will you be okay?"

I squeezed him tight and replied, "I don't know." There was a long pause as I tried to compose myself. I softly said, "It's not going to matter; we are beating this."

He turned to look at me with that smile I will never forget and said, "Thank you for being so good to me! I love you, Jack… promise!"

Chapter Fifty-two

Goodbye 2015, Hello 2016

I was asked the other day, "Are you not so happy to see 2015 come to an end? Wasn't it the worst year of your life?"

Quickly, I responded, "No, not the worst year." I found that question stirred a lot of emotions in me.

As I said goodbye to 2015, I had tears, knowing it was the last year I had with the love of my life. Although 2015 taught me more lessons than I could have imagined, it taught me that if you stand firm and keep the faith, you will get your first stable MRI in the biggest fight of your life. Here are a few of the highlights.

The joy of my oldest daughter winning the Big Sky Championship and living out one of her biggest dreams of competing in the NCAA Regionals came in 2015. It showed me how strong my husband was; chemo treatments in the morning and coaching his high school softball team in the afternoon. If you mentor and coach as Douglas did, great things happen. It brought my middle daughter and youngest a 5A Idaho state title! It was one of the biggest joys in Doug's life, followed by coach of the year.

We were brought down off cloud nine with an MRI showing new tumor growth, which put us living in Seattle for three weeks and going back and forth. I was brought to tears with the graduation of our middle daughter and her heading off to college to live out her dream of playing collegiate softball. The summer was filled with complete happiness and memories being made. Family time was precious to us, the five of us laughed more, shared more, cried more, loved more, and we smiled more. Another champion came to the house, with Demi winning the Idaho State 14U ASA Softball Championship.

A stable MRI in August was shot down in September with the worst possible news. Doug's tumor had spread to the whole right side of his brain. We were reminded to hold onto our faith and enjoy our sweet time as a family. From there, we know how 2015 came to an end.

See, in all these things we experienced, I believe my biggest lesson learned was keeping the faith and seeing the good in all things!

The year tried to break me, but only gave me a broken heart. It tried to tear my family apart, but we were only pushed into a tighter bond. It tried to force me to weakness, but prayer put strength in my body. It confirmed what I have always preached—we have a choice in all things we experience on this journey called life. In 2015, we chose to live, even with every trial thrown in our path, we chose to live.

I could never say 2015 was the worst year because it was the last year I got to spend with my best friend. It gave us many joys, and with every downfall, we became closer, we loved deeper, and we realized how precious time together was.

CaringBridge Entry
December 31, 2015

So as 2015 comes to an end, I would like to say, "Thank you!" In this year, I learned we are not in control. We need to always trust and keep the faith. There are things we will never understand, and if we get stuck trying to figure them out, we are no longer living.

I learned sometimes a simple smile can change a life, that one person's story can touch many lives, because if we share not only the good, but also express the hardships we face, it helps others to not feel alone. I have learned life is limited and we need to seriously live in the moment because in a blink it could be gone.

This past year has challenged me; it has pushed me to breaking points, taken a lot from me, and deeply hurt me. But in the end, here is what I want you, dear reader, to know: *you* have changed me, you have given me a deeper faith, you have provided me with love, you gave me hope, and most of all, you allowed me to have a voice! Thank you.

In 2016, I challenge you all to live. Make it a happier year, even if you don't have anything bringing you joy. You have a choice. You can find something to make you happy.

Love on a deeper level. Do not allow small things to destroy love. Choose to fight for love.

Give from your heart with no stipulations tied to your giving. Giving freely sets you free!

Play more in 2016. We get wrapped up in everyday routines and forget to play! Choose to keep that inner child alive. Plus, watch what happens to your kids and your relationships with your kids if you play more with them.

Speak kinder to those you love, kinder to others, kinder when the doors are shut, and kinder especially to yourself.

See the positive in all situations. It is your choice to either focus on the negative or the positive. Focus on the good, it is what will fill your cup.

Be the best YOU you can be. Do not try to be anyone but yourself.

My wish for 2016 is that it will guide me through this grieving process. May I be filled with hope and joy again. Through my story, I hope I may reach more than before. My wish is for more lessons to be put in front of me—if we are not learning then we are not living. My wish is for strength and compassion to ooze from my pores and to give a light to my girls, for all of us to become pillars of power, and for nothing to stand in our way.

My wish is for more lives to be lived with Christ being the leader and that my sweet girls have a successful, love-filled, lesson-learning, abundant new year! My wish is for 2016 to bless every single soul reading this and that you all feel the power of the Lord.

I wait in anticipation of what you, 2016, will bring me. I ponder what the Lord will guide me to be or what He may guide me to do. I'm excited for this journey filled with many more lessons!

Happy New Year!

Psalms 20:4

May he give you the desire of your heart and make all your plans succeed.

Chapter Fifty-three

Plan B

As time passed, I implemented affirmations into my daily routine that bring my mindset back to the strong positive place it needs to be.

I approve of myself. Today I will see good. These are two simple ones I have used. When we start implementing these in our daily routine the enemy tries to break us by placing negative thoughts in us and trying to cause doubt in what we are affirming. This is where we need to have a strong mindset.

I think of it this way: If we tell ourselves we are sick, even when we are not, if we say it enough times, we start believing it and soon our body is sick. The mind is a powerful tool. We are in control of our thoughts and need to constantly be working on holding on to the positive. Nurture those thoughts as the battle of negative can sneak in. Always know mindset is a choice.

I bought a sign that reads, *Life is all about how you handle Plan B.* It seemed fitting to my journey. I am realizing Plan A is no longer the road I am traveling; I am trying to fit into Plan B. In time, I know I will figure out how Plan B is supposed to look, but for this moment, as fitting as it is, I will say I hate Plan B. I was content with Plan A. I wasn't alone in Plan A. I had my best friend by my side. We had so many things we were going to do in Plan A. I had chosen Plan A; never did I want Plan B.

This is where more of my mindset work comes in. I am a do-it-myself kind of girl. Is it from being an independent person? Stubbornness? Does this trace back to my dad telling us girls that we could do anything we set our minds to? I am not sure; I just know I have always had the thought process of *I do not need any help from anyone, I will figure it out on my own.*

Well, that has slapped me across the face. I am realizing I cannot do this alone. I do need help, and I am struggling to figure it out on my own. With that, I will be starting counseling, hoping to get tools to find my way. Trying to accept it does not mean I am weak because I need someone to help me with my problems and emotions. That is a hard one for the girl who thinks she can do it all herself!

People who know me have come up to me in these past months and asked, "How are you doing?" Before I can even answer, it is usually followed up with, "You look great."

So, do I answer with how I am or say thanks for the compliment? In a millisecond, my head is filled with: *Do I really tell them how I am? Will they be able to handle what I have to say? Do they honestly care?* So, I almost always respond with, "Hanging in there."

I may seem so strong, please understand as a grieving wife, mother, and business owner, I do a superb job of coming across as strong or put together. I do not want to burden others unnecessarily. I also don't want others to feel like they need to solve my problems or make me feel better when I'm not even sure what that would look like. I guess Plan B is a lot of figuring myself out as much as it is figuring life out.

The last two titles, mother and business owner, make it seem as if I am traveling this path of grief with flying colors. In all actuality it is a camouflage to my real self. My girls would not get through this with me curled up in a ball in my closet, and my businesses would not survive if I were not there. That is why I come across as being so strong, when really it is survival mode. That is all I know how to do at this point. Survive.

Grief pretty much rules me.

As much as I thought the tears would lessen, the heartache would fade, and the overwhelming need of Doug's presence would tone down, I have been carelessly wrong. I have hit the ten-month mark without his physical body with me, and I had hoped to be doing better than I actually am.

What do I mean "hoped to be doing better"? What does that even look like? How do I know how I should be or should not be? *Stop comparing yourself to others who have lost loved ones. Stop comparing yourself to others who have felt the loss of Doug. Would you be where you are, and experience what you need to experience?* Oh, that's what I love to hear, telling myself what I tell others. Why is it the advice I give out somehow comes back to repeat in my self-talk?

My days are empty, and my thoughts waver back and forth. I ponder my life alone, and that always brings me to tears.

There is a woman in my life who looks the same, sounds the same, but as I sit there staring at her, I don't know who she is. I've known her all my life, the outer shell looks just like her, but the inside is completely different. It is then I realize I am looking in a mirror.

I keep staring, thinking I will recognize myself, but there is not one thing I can find inside that is the same. I begin to cry. Here I stand looking at myself in a mirror, and I feel like a stranger.

It has been difficult getting to know this new Jacki. She cries a lot and there is a sadness that has filled her. This new Jacki is finding a new strength. She has quieted her voice a bit. She is trying to figure out where she is and how life will be and at the same time, she isn't trying at all. The new has lost the smile, the warrior inside has been shackled, gagged, and bound.

I find glimpses of the old me, but mostly a new version has taken hold. It has become a bit of a challenge for those in my life to figure out this new version of Jacki. As much as some don't like her, I think she is here to stay for a while. I also, at times, don't like her, and it has been a tenuous time with her.

The strength I once had seems to be gone, and those are the days I sit in my jammies in Doug's chair and do nothing. I cry for his presence and his tender touch. I feel like there is no one in my corner anymore. The vast feeling of loneliness consumes me.

At the breaking point of a paralyzing meltdown, I hear his voice. As if he is sitting next to me, he says, "Jack, what is going on? This is not what I want you doing. Pull yourself together!"

I know he would be so angry with all the tears I have shed, and all the time he would say I have *wasted* on missing him. If anything, Doug did not like me fretting over him or worrying about him. So, sitting and shedding tears in the absence of his physical body would have him in an uproar knowing it is about him. In our relationship, Doug hated seeing me sad or upset about anything and would do whatever he had to do to bring my spirits up and make me better.

So back to Plan B. I struggle to find my way. In fact, I have dug my heels in deep. Thanks, but no thanks, I really don't want to do Plan B, plus I have no idea how to survive in Plan B. I knew what Plan A looked like, what Plan A felt like, what expectations Plan A had for me, and Plan A was my comfort.

I'll admit, as good as it feels to have my heels dug in deep, Plan B will blossom into something extraordinary. It is going to take some time to loosen my heels and adjust to it.

When we face any struggle, breakup, debt, job loss, estranged family, empty nest, or rejection—it does not have to be the loss of a loved one—we can find ourselves in the well. After losing Doug and the shock had worn off, I found myself in the bottom of this dark, lonely, and deafeningly quiet space. I sat there by myself, not knowing how I was going to get out of the darkness. How was I going to get through this struggle?

I sat there not knowing how long I would be there or if I was going to be there for the rest of my life. But I knew I had the tools to get out when the time came.

Sitting in the well was a choice for me, and I could shift my mindset and choose to get out of the well. Once I made the decision to work on getting out of the well, I knew I had to rely on prayer. The Lord that had stood by me through this journey would be the one I needed to rely on to help me gain the strength and wisdom to climb out of this well. I found a therapist that I would see twice a week, sometimes to just sit and cry.

It takes a support system to bring you up.

I felt lonely for the fact that my husband was no longer physically present, but I eventually recognized I was not alone. I had friends and family who loved and supported me and kept the momentum going to keep getting up.

Certainly, there were setbacks, but there was an aspiration to get myself out.

I needed to get beyond the grief. I was strong. I'd been strong for all of Doug's cancer and beyond. Many things relied on me to continue, and I couldn't wallow anymore without hurting others. Part of grief is accepting its presence. I believe everyone around me was waiting for me to find that final stage of grief so that I could start implementing the new plan. This was life, and Doug would want me to start living it again too.

Many times, I didn't know if I was ever going to get out of the well, but what I knew was I had the tools to get me out when the time came. These tools are what I came up with as I lived my grief journey.

1. MINDSET—How are you handling and going to pull through this, and what are you going to do with the struggle you are facing? If your mindset is *Poor me, why did this happen to me? I don't know what else to do*, you're done!

You will sit in the well the rest of your life. Find your mindset.

2. CHOICE—Choose to come out of your struggle. Choose to find your strength to become better. Choose what you are going to do with the struggle and choose for yourself above all others.

   There were moments in my journey I had to re-use this tool. In the emergency room the first night when we got the news there was a lesion on Doug's brain, we chose to fight and not allow whatever we were about to face to define us.

   Again, when we were in the depths of Doug's fight for his life, I recall an intimate conversation he and I had. There were many tears shed during this time, but we made the choice we would not be victims in our story. We wanted to come out victors and share our story along the way.

   Never would I tell you this is easy. Finding the power within to choose good when all around you feels like it is caving in on you isn't the simple choice. Choosing to see the positive or the lesson coming from what you are facing took a strength that was led by faith.

   Once I lost Douglas, it took me a long while to realize I needed to implement this tool again in my journey. Was I going to allow the grief I was facing, the pain of a shattered heart I was experiencing, to do exactly what he and I said we wouldn't do—play the victim? *No.* That is when I chose to live again.

   I encourage you as you are facing struggles in your life, as hard as it may be, make the choice to be the **VICTOR** of your story, not the victim.

3. FAITH—I had the Lord and knew my faith in Him would help get me through. He would be by my side, and with

prayer, I trusted He had the ability to guide me to where I needed to be.

Having faith through your struggle does not imply it will be a breeze, it means you have trust or confidence in something. It means that through your struggle, you have strong belief.

4. SUPPORT—This one may be scary, but if you cannot do it on your own, you may need the help. Surround yourself with the encouraging, uplifting, energetic souls who will be by your side. Aunt Nancy, otherwise known as Negative Nancy, is not who we want to surround ourselves with.

We need to surround ourselves with loved ones that will not only sit with us in our struggle but will build us up and carry us when we need the strength.

When we are in the depths of the well and cannot find it in us to get out, we need stronger guidance and that will come from a therapist, pastor, or doctor. There are also self-help books, motivational speakers, podcasts, and possibly some sort of medicine. I was listening to a motivational speaker give a talk and they made a statement: "Life is not happening *to* you it is happening *for* you."

As soon as I heard it, it was as if I was slapped across the face. All the things that had been happening in my life were preparing me for this. Life was happening for me, preparing.

In moments of struggle, we want to question, *Why? Why now? Why so much? Why me?* It should be, *What can I learn? What am I gaining?* Sometimes that is very hard to understand when we are in the middle of our struggle.

After losing Doug, my general practitioner said to consider taking some anti-anxiety meds. Not only did it help with the anxiety I was feeling, but it helped me with my sleep. I was closed off to taking meds at first but came around to it.

5. HOPE—This is simply facing what is in front of us and having a desire for a specific thing to occur. Hope is a constant that helps provide a peace as we travel through hard times. It means believing good things will develop by holding onto our faith. Hope is finding the positive in any situation and looking at adversity as an opportunity to learn.

Through our journey, we held tightly to hope until his last breath. Hope will bring you to see that no matter where you are, life continues, and brighter days appear.

Once again, I will say I had moments of letting my hope fade, but I never let it get too far from me. When I realized hope didn't have to be my own thoughts or my doings, that I could have hope in the Lord and he would carry my burdens, I felt better.

Isaiah 40:31

But those who hope in the Lord will renew their strength. They will soar on wings like eagles; they will run and not grow weary, they will walk and not be faint.

Chapter Fifty-four

In Time, It Has Become Harder

Blog Post on Website
October 2016

In every meltdown and in conversations, I have been told to be patient and that in time it will get easier. I'm told that as time goes by, the ache gets less, the healing starts, and the bleeding wound will begin to form a scar. *This has not been true on my journey!*

As time has gone by, my aching body has gotten worse, my tears have overflowed, and the missing of Doug's presence has intensified. For the souls who might be saying "this is unhealthy," well, in your circumstances it may be unhealthy, but on my journey, this is what I am doing.

I have come to terms with the fact loved ones don't like seeing us hurt and have their own vision of how and where we need to be on our grief journeys. Google can even tell us what "step/stage" we should or need to be in. Of the things I have witnessed through my grief, every single person does it differently. Trust me, four souls live in this house, three raised the same, and guess what? All four are going through the process in their own unique way.

Oh, it's been hell because I have done my best to have them grieve as I am. It has exploded in my face, caused me more tears and heartache, and made me realize how they are doing it, what they are feeling, is perfect for what *they* need. How they do it and how I am doing it is not the right way or the wrong way. It is the way each soul needs to do it to get to the new place on their journeys.

I was completely startled one evening when I was holding Bentli, sobbing, missing her dad. She screamed, "I just want Dad, I want Dad to hold me!"

I began crying with her and said, "I know, sis, me too!"

In the sweetest voice, she said, "Mom, you don't understand exactly what I'm going through, the only ones who truly know what I'm going through are Z and Demi. Just like we don't know what you are honestly going through."

Correct, she was absolutely correct! I had compared myself to other women who had lost their husbands. I had questioned myself, beat myself up, and even had extensive self-talks. Finally, I came to the realization that how I am doing it is exactly how I need to be. I allowed opinions to be spoken to me, statistics shared with me, advice on how to be doing it, but I realized I should only listen and not absorb it; I realized I should not take it on. My grief journey was my own. I vowed to write this story all by myself and heal in my own way.

Regarding the statement "in time it gets easier," my grief got harder as time went by. With the help of my counselor, I began slowly learning what the tornado inside of me consisted of. I didn't have *only* the grief of losing my best friend swirling in there. There were numerous particles mixed in, causing pain. I lost a voice. I lost relationships. I lost loved ones and friendships. I lost an identity I had for years. I lost a bit of my faith. I lost my plan. I lost all my joy. There were more particles to the mixture, but my goodness, I could write pages of all the items ripping my insides to shreds.

I noticed in September it was getting harder. I was confused by what I was feeling. I chalked it up as the time of the year—part of the journey. Then, I recognized what was happening. I began reliving the past two and a half years in my head. Was it because it brought me close to Doug or was this a malfunction in my grief journey? Because when I started doing it, I could see it as if I was in it, I could smell every single scent I encountered, I could hear every voice spoken to me at appointments or near me. I felt all the energies and emotions as if it was happening in that exact moment.

I pondered over and over whether this was healthy, if I needed to find a way to stop, and then it became clear to me, as if the Lord said, "Now, child, you may experience it all."

In March of 2014, I went into warrior mode. It was fight or flight, and I was fighting. Through our journey with cancer, I wasn't backing down to anything. I remember one appointment in particular.

The doctor walked in and said, "Good morning, how are you feeling, Doug?"

"I feel pretty good."

"You look good."

Then the testing. "Hold your arms out straight and touch your nose with your finger; pull my arms; push against my arms; lift your leg; now the other leg; watch my finger; look straight at me and tell me which fingers I have pointed up; spell *world*; what is today?"

He finished testing like a champ and then the words were spoken, "It looks as if there is growth."

Doug turned to me with the look of complete fear. I quickly and firmly stated, "We are good. We have options. No need to panic. We are fine."

As we left, he started in with all the questions. "Jack, what do you think, what did this or that mean?"

I continually spoke strength over him, I never broke.

That is just one appointment I speak of; I have relived every single one we went to for twenty months. But now, I am *not* the warrior,

I am the little girl who lived inside of me scared to death when I heard *new growth*, *more spots*, and *treatment didn't work*. And when he turned to me with *scared to death* all over his face, I began to cry.

I have relived every moment from September to present, allowing that little girl to be scared to death and cry as many tears as she needed. When I went into warrior mode, I pushed that little girl down and put a heavy lid on her so she wouldn't come out. Slowly, carefully, I began feeling those moments as raw as if I were there.

And in doing this, I also allowed her to grieve the loss of being a caregiver. Reliving it has caused massive tears to flow and feeling the pain as I did was excruciating. As a result, I found a slice of the healing process.

November 2, 2016

The numbness takes over the body after the shock subsides. The body completely protects itself, without you consciously knowing it. The lifting of the numbness causes tremendous pain.

Think about when your foot or hand goes to sleep and the blood supply finally starts filling back in, that prickling sensation you feel. It is like that but a billion times stronger. But to get the feeling back in your foot or hand, you have to endure the sensation. My grief is the same: As the numbness begins to lift, I am starting to feel, which in turn, means there is more pain.

It becomes especially hard when my psyche gets to me. I find myself feeling as if everyone's life seems to be going on, which I know it is, but mine isn't. I think it's because I am not sure how to keep going right now, or maybe I don't want to.

The hardest is feeling as if I am on an island alone surrounded by thousands. You can be surrounded by many but still feel completely isolated. It is like standing alone in a glass box looking out at the world, screaming at the top of my lungs, and no one hearing my words. The loneliness of being the surviving spouse is, to me, almost unbearable.

I can remember years ago, way before Doug got sick, having a conversation about death with him. I specifically said, "I have to go first because the thought of living without you, I'm pretty sure I couldn't do." My soul was correct, I'm struggling trying to do it.

I felt I had been walking this path smoothly, but I came to a fork in my path. Two doors were presented, and I took the one on the right. I walked through it and slammed the door shut. Complete darkness. I am standing in complete darkness. I turned to go back out, and the door is locked. So now, I am standing in the dark absolutely paralyzed, hoping somehow a candle can be lit for me to see where I need to be going. But until I figure out how to light a candle, I will stand here in the darkest of dark, allowing it to be okay to be here.

The one-year anniversary is approaching and the mother hen in me has managed to round up my chicks to have home with me this weekend. Blessed am I to have those three girls!

Psalm 56:8

You've kept track of my every toss and turn through sleepless nights, each tear entered in your ledger, each ache written in your book. (From the YouVersion Bible app.)

Chapter Fifty-five

Faith

Blog Post
Early 2017

I stand firm in my faith, I hold prayer high, and I have always trusted in His plan, but lately I sit in silence wanting to have Christ hear my words, and for the first time in my life, not one word comes out of me. I have always been so connected in my prayers, and here I am with nothing. There is so much I want to say, but there is silence, only silence. *Where have my words gone, why won't I speak any?*

It is the time I need Christ the most, and I cannot get myself to stretch my hand out to Him. I question myself, maybe my faith wasn't as strong as I thought. Please don't get me wrong, faith is still inside me, somewhere. It's just a bit lost at this moment.

I quickly realized my mortal mind is confused; God is for us, but I have never felt pain like this. Trust in the Lord, but you took my babies' daddy too early. God knows best, but I don't know how to live without Douglas. God hears our cries; well, He should be sick of me because I do it a lot.

I am going to do this grieving journey like I have always lived my life, I am going to do it my way. It might not fit the stages/steps of grieving. It may not even look like the best process. And I know I will grieve for the rest of my life. I can truly see myself grieving forever because of the intensity of the love I continue to have for Douglas.

God patiently waits, sitting with us in our sorrow. He never leaves our side even when we may not feel Him. Having faith is knowing when we struggle, we don't have to carry it all on our own. The Lord is so gracious when He takes our burdens, yet we must be willing to give them to him. Why feel like we need to carry them ourselves? There is no award given for carrying all the weight of our struggle.

I yearn for the day I feel pure joy back in my body. I patiently wait for my smile to be back and shining on others. I am believing it will happen, all in due time.

1 Corinthians 13:13

And now these three remain: faith, hope and love.
But the greatest of these is love.

Faith is knowing that when my life is in an uproar and I feel in a tailspin, it won't be devastation. I can trust in the wisdom of the Lord. Having faith in these times allows us to breathe, to take a step away, and to know we will be okay. Faith is what lives inside of us that keeps our light shining in the darkest of days. It is possible to only have a mustard seed size of trust in the Lord.

For my journey, it took me praying and reading my Bible to strengthen my faith when I felt it weakening. Plus, I give grace to myself because I had moments when I chose to *not* have faith (or maybe it was having it, just not acknowledging it).

I was allowing my grief and heartache to run my everything. When we face struggles in our lives, there are many occasions when we doubt the faith we believed we had. I will be the first to tell you, that is okay! Because we hold doubt does not mean we leave our faith or it leaves us. It means we are facing hard things and can't find it within us.

Once again, I say give yourself grace. Grace has been my lifesaver more times than not. Start using it with yourself.

Chapter Fifty-six

Oh, My Love

Blog Post
March 26, 2017

Dear Doug,

I have lived sixteen months and twenty days without your physical body next to me. It has tried me, taught me, changed me; it has made me numb and made me feel. It has been the hardest sixteen months and twenty days of my life.

It had been close to a year and a half since I slept in our bed, where I snuggled you in my arms. I finally found the courage to take my broken-down body back to our bed. The lights and TV were left on as I lay there sobbing. Another discomfort of my grief, I had no idea the bed we shared could be so frightening; now it scares the living shit out of me.

It has been three-and-a-half weeks since I started trying to sleep in our bed, and each night still brings on a bit of anxiety. Although I have turned the lights off—okay, let's be real, I have downsized to a nightlight—the TV still runs. The warmth of our bed is no longer there, but I'm slowly finding comfort lying where we shared many intimate moments. Memories engulf me of snuggling, solving the world's problems, planning our future, and expressing what we both wanted for our three girls. I am sorry for taking advantage of our bedtime conversations and possibly falling asleep as you spoke. What I would give to have those sometimes-meaningless conversations again.

Today, we would be celebrating our twenty-fourth wedding anniversary. As I sit here this evening, I remember the night before our wedding, the rehearsal dinner with both our families and friends. Anxious for the next day, you kissed me goodnight and said, "I can't wait to see you tomorrow." You paused for a moment and finished, "Jack, I love you and can't wait to spend the rest of my life with you!"

Oh, my love, you got to spend the rest of your life with me! I am so grateful I fell in love with you at fifteen when everyone thought I was crazy. I am beyond thankful I married you at nineteen and spent the best, most trying, mountain climbing, smooth sailing, love-filled twenty-two-plus years with you.

Today, I want you to know all the while we were together, both in our physical bodies, you had been preparing me for the future. I had no idea you were doing it at the time. As my head is starting to clear, I'm seeing all the things you knew I would need to know to survive without you, to continue to grow our girls and to run a successful business.

Douglas, my love, today I want to thank you for loving me the way you did, for walking beside me as my life partner, never in front nor behind. You encouraged me when I needed it, and you reeled me in when I also needed it but didn't know it.

My love, you blessed me with three amazing girls you fathered like every dad should. You instilled in those babies a zest for life, strength, and a belief in themselves no matter what others said or thought of them. You provided them a comfort I'm finding I don't have. They have taken on your need for shoes, your habit of keeping your cars clean, your smart-ass remarks, your love and protection of me, and your amazing smile. Thank you for being such a fabulous dad for such a short period.

As my heart still aches for you, and I miss you every single day, it is seeing you come through those girls that brings me peace.

Happy Anniversary Douglas! I loved you first, I loved you the longest, but you always said you loved me the mostest!

Love you... Promise!

Chapter Fifty-seven

Where Have You Been...

Blog Post
October 2018

Oh, I have been fighting a battle within. I have been trapped in darkness. I have been traveling my journey alone, by my own choice. I've been extremely mad; in fact, this is the maddest I have ever been in my life.

I chose to not speak to the Lord anymore. I dug my feet in deep, my stubbornness was in full force. I had my mind made up; I was doing this journey on my own. I had trusted You for so long, and I concluded *not* to put my trust in You. I was in control of myself, my choices, and my situations. That is where I have been.

The Lord replied,

Dearest Jacki,

Do you believe you walked in darkness alone? Do you think your anger blocked me? Do you think you weren't doing work? Do you think the platform I have given you was ripped out from underneath you? I, my sweet child, have actually held you on some of the darkest days you have been traveling. That was not you, but me. You may have cussed me, spoke of anger toward me, but I have only loved you.

Your anger has not affected my relationship with you. I have only been by your side waiting patiently for the light you used to shine to be back and burning bright. Although you feel you have not been doing my work, oh child of mine, do not be deceived; you have continually been doing my work. We have been planting things within you that will only be magnified when you are ready. That platform you speak of I have always known you would step back on, but with a fire inside that would allow you to reach more people. I know deep in your faith you believe trusting me and my plans will only prosper you. That confusion will be cleared in due time.

This is a conversation I have had! Here is what I now know. It doesn't matter where you are, what you are going through, or how hurt you may feel, the Lord will always, always, ALWAYS, not sometimes but ALWAYS be with you, loving you, holding you, guiding you, and being faithful to you! Even if you aren't ready or don't want to feel it!

My journey is taking a shift and I am super excited where we are headed! I am grateful I can share it and possibly one soul may be inspired! So, to that one soul, go ahead and dig your heels, go ahead and be angry, go ahead and think you can do it on your own because patiently on the sideline, your sideline, the Lord awaits!

Epilogue

Over six years have passed since I lost Douglas. Before he died, he talked about how he would place signs in our paths once he was gone, signs of support that he was still with us.

Many times, I walked away from our conversations with so much admiration for the man I fell in love with. Other times, I walked away sick to my stomach, knowing we were having end-of-life conversations. I am grateful that we had the opportunity to speak the words we did.

I frequent the cemetery, and on one particular day, shortly after the funeral, I had an amazing encounter. It was one of the harder days I had experienced with lots of tears. I remember sitting there mumbling, "I can't do this… I can't do this without you." Trying to catch my breath, I heard a Canadian goose honking softly close to me. I looked up and saw a single goose walking about twenty yards from me. I began crying hysterically.

I threw my face into my hands and as hard as it was to get the words out, I cried out: "Douglas! Douglas! Douglas!" The goose stayed for about twenty minutes and every few minutes, it honked. It was the sign I needed at that moment. Of course, it was this exquisite bird that Douglas used to hunt. This is the bird that would be the sign that he was still close to me.

From that day on, there have been many times I needed a bit of comfort, needed to feel him close, or to give me reassurance he is doing okay; sometimes it's when I am struggling or missing Doug. Every single time, a goose will fly overhead and honk.

These signs are a deep layer of comfort that soothes my heart, brings some relief to my hurt, and places a smile on my face.

Douglas will always be with me.

Grief is the most astonishing adventure I have ever traveled. I gave myself all the time I needed to be in the pit of sadness. But I knew, in the depth of my sorrow, the sun still came up each morning, and there was a life to live, to do amazing things.

I felt the hurt, the anguish, and the complete sense of emptiness that had filled my body. I hung on by this little string of hope that, in due time, life would be restored in me, and that I wouldn't be just going through the motions for there was a purpose that I need to complete.

I prayed for healing, for the utmost powerful surge to be put on my heart to have the pieces bandaged back together and that the fog occupying my brain would be lifted, and clarity would fill it. I learned that faking it made it easier for others around me. But not for me.

In the grief journey, remember to focus on yourselves; do not let outside grief consume your journey. Grief is different for everyone, how they handle it, how they express it, and how it is taken. I had to learn it would be selfish to think everyone needed to be on the same grieving track as myself. This included my three beautiful girls.

During the darkest days of grief, I knew I would not allow the darkness to settle in my heart. Here is where grace joined my journey, aware of where I was in my grief but believing I would one day find the path to greatness where joy would again fill every ounce of my being, and Christ would, once again, beam from my smile, my touch, and my voice.

Psalms 34:18

The Lord is close to the brokenhearted and saves those who are crushed in spirit.

Please understand, I wept for Douglas and my heart ached for his presence, but I always knew the Lord was by my side.

I walked through days where it was hard to feel, and I struggled to remember what a joyful life was. My joy was filled with Douglas, which made the tears flow down my face and my heart ache. I questioned if I would ever feel joy again.

I tried to process this extremely hard time in my life. I knew it was going to take a long time to find my new normal. I decided I would not put an exact time on myself to go through grief; see, you cannot do that to a broken heart. For those twenty months of our journey, it was me, the power of strength, the rock of the family, the extreme fighter I would not want to meet in a dark alley, who had held it together, never swaying from what I stood for. I never allowed myself to even think about starting to grieve the slowly failing health of my husband.

I had twenty-four seven with Douglas by my side, and complete loneliness intensified the grief I felt once he'd passed.

Baby steps, baby steps are what I told myself to take. When I couldn't catch my breath, I relied on strength I have always had. I gave myself permission, when I found my heart aching to the point of sickness, to lie in the arms of Jesus for comfort. When tears streamed down my face and I couldn't stop them, I vowed to let them flow like a raging river. It was a release that needed to be experienced.

The love, the bond, and the time I had with my best friend and husband will forever live on. Through my actions, my three girls, and the life I will now live, Doug will be honored.

Patience is my word of choice. I will have patience as I travel this journey of grief. Christ will be patient with me as I work through the challenges of grief, and I will, in the end, be filled with a new understanding, a new joy, a deeper relationship, and a great curriculum to share!

Matthew 5:4

Blessed are those who mourn, for they will be comforted.

Jacki Corta

Jacki Corta is an Idaho native and successful entrepreneur of thirty years. She's also a grief mentor and motivational speaker, sharing her story of overcoming adversity, finding her strength, and keeping the faith. Her brand, Strength > Struggle™, was created to remind the people of the world no matter the struggle you face, your strength is greater than that struggle.

Jacki's undeniable strength attracts her audiences, leaving them with a new outlook on the challenges they may be facing.

She is a momma to three grown daughters and loves being Mimi to her grandbabies. Follow Jacki on social media @jackicorta

For more great books from WEX Press
Visit Books.GracePointPublishing.com

If you enjoyed reading *When Your Miracle Doesn't Come*, and purchased it
through an online retailer, please return to the site and write a review to help
others find the book.

Made in the USA
Coppell, TX
12 September 2023

21535785R00144